THE GILL HISTORY OF IRELAND

General Editors: JAMES LYDON, PH.D.
MARGARET MACCURTAIN, PH.D.

Other titles in the series

IRELAND IN THE LATER MIDDLE AGES

James Lydon

GILL AND MACMILLAN

Published by
Gill and Macmillan Ltd
2 Belvedere Place
Dublin 1
and internationally through
association with
Macmillan Publishers Limited

Cover design by Cor Klaasen

7171 0563 6

Printed and bound in the Republic of Ireland by the
Richview Press Limited, Dublin

Contents

Foreword

Preface

Prologue

For my friends in Wicklow

Foreword

THE study of Irish history has changed greatly in recent decades as more evidence becomes available and new insights are provided by the growing number of historians. It is natural, too, that with each generation new questions should be asked about our past. The time has come for a new large-scale history. It is the aim of the Gill History of Ireland to provide this. This series of studies of Irish history, each written by a specialist, is arranged chronologically. But each volume is intended to stand on its own and no attempt has been made to present a uniform history. Diversity of analysis and interpretation is the aim; a group of young historians have tried to express the view of their generation on our past. It is the hope of the editors that the series will help the reader to appreciate in a new way the rich heritage of Ireland's history.

JAMES LYDON, PH.D.
MARGARET MACCURTAIN, PH.D.

Preface

THIS is a history of Anglo-Ireland in the later middle ages. Gaelic Ireland is dealt with only in so far as it impinged on the other. Such a limited treatment can only be excused on the ground of limited space and the present inadequate state of our knowledge of Gaelic Ireland (though the publication of K. Nicholls' *Gaelic and Gaelicised Ireland* in this series shows that a real breakthrough is at hand). It can be argued, too, that separate treatment of the two cultures and two communities is legitimate, since they remained apart until the end of the middle ages, whatever assimilation had taken place at certain levels of society and in certain places. I have tried in the first two chapters to give an account of society and the institutions of government. The restriction of space has meant that too much had to be left out, especially in the first chapter. But half a loaf is better than none.

I would like to thank Mrs Thomas Sullivan who patiently typed a crabbed and difficult manuscript, and the long-suffering Mr Ray O Farrell, of Gill and Macmillan, who was kindness itself during a very difficult period for me. I am also grateful to Professor A. J. Otway-Ruthven of Trinity College, Dublin, who allowed me to make use of her map in *A history of Medieval Ireland*. Finally, the dedication makes it plain where my main thanks are due. Any value this book may have is the result of the many courtesies and kindnesses I have received here in Wicklow.

Knocknadroose, 1973.

Prologue
'The Conquest Limpeth'

IN October 1318, Edward Bruce, king of Ireland and brother of King Robert I of Scotland, was killed in a minor battle at Faughart, just north of Dundalk. His death was greeted with approval by most of the Irish annalists: he was 'the common ruin of the Galls and Gaels of Ireland' and 'never was there a better deed done for the men of Ireland than this, since the beginning of the world and the banishing of the Fomorians from Ireland'. No wonder the Irish rejoiced, for his death marked the end of a traumatic experience in the life of the island, when 'falsehood and famine and homicide filled the country'. The invasion of the Scots in 1315 was seen in retrospect to have been a disaster for Gaelic and Anglo-Irish alike: this 'warlike army caused the whole of Ireland to tremble, both Gall and Gael'. The war caused destruction in many parts of the country, with armies passing to and fro, burning and looting as they went: 'between them they left neither wood nor lea nor corn nor crop nor stead nor barn nor church, but fired and burnt them all'. Official records, too, chronicle the destruction of war—there are many references on the Irish chancery rolls to lands laid waste in Meath, Dublin, Kildare, Cork, Limerick, Tipperary and Louth.

In the confusion of battles, local vendettas were pursued and many old scores were settled, adding to the horror of those years. The internecine strife among the O Connors, for example, gave rise to many atrocities, as when an O Kelly sided with an O Connor in pursuit of a Mac

Dermot and another O Connor, following them to Glendarragh in county Sligo, 'where they killed many thousand cows and sheep and horses. At that time they stripped women and ruined children and lowly folk, and never within the memory of men were so many cattle fruitlessly destroyed in one place'. To make matters even worse, these were years of great famine, common to the whole of Europe, the result of crop failure because of 'intolerable, destructive bad weather' and there were 'numerous wonderful diseases throughout all Erinn' and 'a destruction of people in great numbers'.

The Bruce invasion of Ireland, then, had ended in disaster. Coupled with the effects of the famine which hit Ireland at the same time, it had a shattering impact on the whole of Ireland, Gaelic and Anglo-Irish. Some parts of the country were depopulated and laid waste, never to recover fully in the middle ages. The rule of law broke down in places, feudatories broke faith, and the government found control slipping from its grasp. The treason of the lords gave point to the ever growing problem of the 'rebel English' and the taking of hostages (as in 1318, when the sons of Eustace le Poer and Richard Tuit were sent to England) was no answer. The events of the invasion, too, highlighted the growing weakness of the central government and accelerated the break-up of the feudal settlement which had already manifested itself before the end of the thirteenth century. The military problem posed by Leinster worsened, the precarious financial position of the government reached critical proportions, and the Gaelic revival continued to grow in strength.

For Gaelic Ireland the invasion was not the catalyst it might have been. The final condemnations of the annalists were a far cry from the hopes raised by King Robert of Scotland, when he wrote to 'each and every king of Ireland, the prelates, too, and the clergy and inhabitants of all Ireland, our friends', telling them that he had sent messengers to 'treat with each and every one of you, in our name, about a perpetual confederation of special friendship between us and you . . . by which, God willing, our nation (i.e. the Scots and Irish) may be restored to its ancient liberty'. When he himself landed in Ireland he came, according to the *Annals of Loch Cé*, 'to expel the Foreigners from Erinn'. But instead, the confusion of wars in Ireland was only made worse. And if some Gaelic areas succeeded in making use of the wars to recover 'ancient liberty', in other parts the feudal settlement was restored with remarkable speed. There was to be no foreign deliverer and Gaelic Ireland was left as fragmented politically as it had been before. Never again, while the medieval lordship lasted, was an attempt made to unite the Gaeil and expel the Gaill. The two communities were left to confront one another, two distinct cultures which were naturally antagonistic to each other. There was a degree of assimilation, so that at times in some places the distinction was blurred. But they remained locked in hostility to the end and folk memory, epitomised by the use of such epithets as 'Old English' and 'Old Irish' by later generations, kept alive the feeling of difference. In some respects it has lasted down to the present day.

The conquest of Ireland by the Anglo-Normans, which had seemed so secure and permanent in the thirteenth century, was clearly beginning to collapse by the time of the Bruce invasion. By then, as the chancellor Gerrard expressed it in the sixteenth century, 'the quiet estate wherein the land had long remained began to decay'. He put it even more trenchantly when he said that 'the estate became thus tattered'. The story of Ireland in the later middle ages is largely the story of how some pieces of the shattered conquest were held together.

Italian map of Ireland, *c.* 1339.

1 Land and People

The land of Ireland

Ireland in the middle ages lay at the very edge of the known world, outside the main trade routes and difficult of access. A sea crossing in those days before the compass could be a terrifying experience and ships hugged the coast as much as possible. In the late fourteenth century a Spanish pilgrim to Lough Derg chartered a boat at Chester, followed the coast as far as Holyhead and then set sail for Dublin. But it was the Isle of Man that first loomed into sight. From there, as he tells it himself, 'I crossed with good weather and arrived in Ireland at the end of some days' tacking'. Even with good weather, then, a crossing was not easy; bad weather could mean long delays. A writer of a letter in 1255 describes a wait of nine days on the Welsh coast for fair weather before he could set out for Ireland. Then he endured 'tempests for three days and three nights at sea' before reaching Wexford. A letter from Edward I to Geoffrey de Geneville in January 1274 again highlights the dangers and the delays. Letters of protection had been sent to Ireland, the king writes. 'One of the bearers of the letters, which were in duplicate owing to the dangers of the sea, perished by shipwreck, and the other was so delayed that he could not arrive in time'. To be caught at sea in a storm nearly always meant misfortune and there is a long catalogue of distinguished people drowned between Ireland and England.

Foreigners, therefore, were naturally loath to come to

Ireland. Even though St Patrick's Purgatory in Lough Derg enjoyed widespread fame in Europe, attracting pilgrims from as far away as Hungary, it was (as one of them put it) 'at the ends of the world in Ireland, which is the most ultimate province of the western world'. Europeans were incredibly ignorant of Ireland. The distinguished and learned cardinal Guillaume Fillastre kept a famous diary during the council of Constance, which recorded that there were 'four great kingdoms in Ireland, near England, namely Connacht, Galway, Munster and Meath' and that it contained 'more than 60 wide and spacious dioceses'. Even the Italian cartographers, who show a surprising knowledge of some parts of the Irish coastline, were hopelessly inaccurate in their attempts to depict the main geographical features of Ireland. This lack of knowledge, which of course extended to Englishmen as well, coupled with the problems of slow and difficult communications, must have been a severe handicap to all chief governors in their efforts to plan military operations.

Among the foreigners who did manage to get to Ireland, none was more observant or curious than Gerald de Barry (Cambrensis), who left a vivid description of the land and its wonders at the end of the twelfth century. He saw a landscape of woods and bogs and he remarked in particular on the large number of lakes. 'The land is fruitful', he wrote, 'and rich in its fertile soil and plentiful harvests. Crops abound in the fields, flocks on the mountains, and wild animals in the woods'. The climate was 'the most temperate of all countries. Cancer does not here drive you to take shade from its burning heat; nor does the cold of Capricorn send you rushing to the fire'. Rain was frequent, keeping grass green the whole year round. Cattle were everywhere in great herds. There were wild animals in abundance, so that a multiplicity of skins and furs was available for export. Gerald mentions the great numbers of hawks, falcons and sparrow-hawks to be seen, which were much sought after in England up to the end of the middle ages. Altogether, he describes a land which had a great agricultural potential, even if he is scathing about the lack of interest shown by Gaelic Ireland in developing these natural resources.

The manors

It was the Anglo-Norman settlers who were to exploit the riches which the land of Ireland provided. After the early invaders conquered land, they settled and then cleared it, making it productive so that not only were the settlements largely self-supporting, but they were soon producing a surplus for market. This was done in the first place by planting manors all over the conquered land. It must be remembered that most of the early invaders were French-speaking and they naturally brought with them French feudalism, modified by English custom. Land was divided into fiefs, held of the king by tenants-in-chief. Service, usually of a military nature, was rendered by these tenants. The great lordship of Meath, for example, had been held by de Lacy for a service of fifty knights. Other feudal incidents were involved in such tenure, such as the giving of counsel, the payment of financial aids on certain occasions, rights of marriage, wardships and escheats.

The major tenants-in-chief subinfeudated their great fiefs. There was continuous division of lordships among lesser tenants, all of whom were enmeshed in a system of feudal relationships involving fealty, services and often rents as well. Many tenants held only tiny parcels of land, such as John Morris who in an exchequer record of 1340 was described as the 'farmer of a third part of two parts of the manor'. Others held entire manors. All were required to do service of one kind or another for their lands. These varied widely, even if most of them were military. Knight service, the most common, had been largely commuted into a money payment by the later middle ages. Other

3

kinds of service, largely of a formal character symbolising a dependent tenure, remained fixed. For example, the manor of Lucan was held for a tabour and four pairs of furred gloves annually, that of Dalkey for one hawk.

Each manor was a largely self-supporting unit and naturally there was considerable variety in organisation from one place to another. But generally the tenants were divided into two main classes, the free and the unfree. The latter were betaghs (*betagii*), who were of servile status and formed an essential and important element in the population of the manor. Before the invasion, the typical commoner was the biatach, in free possession of his land but owing services (usually involving labour of one kind or another) to his lord. The Anglo-Normans naturally equated this with the status of the serf on their own manors, who owed labour services and was tied to the land. So the biatach became the *betagius*, became unfree and tied to the manor. One of the provisions of the Treaty of Windsor in 1175 was that those betaghs who had become refugees during the invasion should now be compelled to return to their lands. Presumably like all refugees they were only too glad to return home and it does not seem that their reduction in status was any great hindrance. At any rate, they appear in substantial numbers on most manors later, usually holding large blocks of land jointly. Materially they were much better off than the cottars, who usually held only about half an acre and were also burdened with labour services, together with a small annual rent.

The free tenants were by far the most important and the wealthiest element on any manor. Many owed military service, usually commuted to a money payment ('royal service' as it was called in Ireland). Others paid a money rent. All held their tenure in perpetuity. They had to attend the lord's court and were liable to the other customary feudal incidents. There were also farmers, holding land for a fixed time by lease, paying rent. On many manors

4

were the gavillers, a class of tenant peculiar to Ireland, who were tenants at will. In addition to paying rent, they usually owed labour services. By far the most interesting class of tenant, found on very many manors, were the burgesses. Rural boroughs seem to have been a peculiarity of the feudal structure of Ireland and there seems to be little doubt that burgage tenure was offered as an inducement to attract settlers to Ireland (just as the light labour services required from tenants, by comparison with England, was another attraction). At any rate the burgesses formed a distinct community on many manors, holding their burgages at a low rent, with their own court and other privileges besides.

An extent of the manor of Cloncurry in county Kildare, made in November 1304, gives a good idea of the population of a normal manor. Forty-three free tenants are listed, holding parcels of land varying in size from one knight's fee to a single house in the village of Cloncurry. There were 112 burgesses holding two ploughlands (or 240 acres – the equivalent of about 600 modern statute acres, since the medieval acre was about two and a half times the size of the modern one). They paid 112s. in rent and had their own court, the hundred. Next come the farmers, over forty of them, holding tenements varying from one plough-land and 20 acres (for £11.3.6 annually on a seven year lease) to half an acre (10d. per annum on a yearly lease). There are 63 betaghs, holding jointly 34½ acres of land and two more holding a cottage and half an acre each. Eleven gavillers are listed, all holding cottages and tiny parcels of land. Finally come 42 cottars, each with a cottage and a small plot, paying 2d. to 4d. annually.

It is striking that there were no labour services attached to any of the tenements at Cloncurry. The manor depended on paid service and the first part of the extent lists the cost of seasonable operations: 'the weeding of an acre costs one penny and the cost of mowing, tying and stooking in the field of an acre of wheat is 10 pence, and of an acre of oats is

8 pence, and the cost of carting and stacking in the haggard and the thatching of the stack is 3 pence per acre. And the cost of threshing a crannock of wheat is about 2 pence and of threshing a crannock of oats is 2 pence. And 5 crannocks of wheat and of oats can be winnowed for 1 penny . . . And each driver and carter gets for his wages 6 shillings per annum. And the bird-scarer gets 4 shillings and the sower gets the same as the bird-scarer'.

On most manors labour services were common, even if they were much less onerous than those customary in England. The legislation of 1299 shows how important such services could be. It was commonly complained that the ploughmen, threshers, carters and others were refusing customary services 'on account of the fertility of the year'. Consequently the council enacted that such services were to be rendered and that no lord should offer higher wages than were normal, or try to attract labour from other manors. This year had seen great harvests and consequently there was a shortage of labour. Wages naturally shot up, hence the reluctance of tenants to perform customary services for low wages. Such services were too valuable to be let go lightly. At Grangegorman, for example, services were attached to most tenements. A rental of 1326 lists John Catt with certain holdings, for which he pays 35s. yearly. 'And he shall plough, at winter seed time, and Lent, for four days, or shall give 6d. And he shall carry, in harvest, with his cart, the corn of the lord, for two days. And the said works are worth 6d. a year'. The services had already been commuted to a money payment. Grange-gorman was held by Holy Trinity, Dublin. In the account of the seneschal of the priory for 1339, there is an expenditure of 2s. 1½d. 'in hoeing the corn of Grange Gorman this year', and of £8.5.3¼ 'in the harvesting of all corn growing this year in the manor of Gorman'. The seneschal in 1343 accounts for a wide variety of labour costs – the wages of smiths, carpenters, reapers, threshers, carters, ploughmen, thatchers, servants and workers of all kinds. There was 'a certain medical man' paid 15d. for healing and curing oxen (used for ploughing – the typical plough team was 8 oxen) and farm horses. Butter 'for anointing the necks of oxen, and healing and curing farm horses' cost 21d.; sulphur, for the same, 3½d. A certain Thomas of Ashbourne was paid 7d. and board for 7 days 'thatching 3 stacks of oats, 1 long stack of peas, raking and preparing four great stacks of wheat lest the rain should get in'. At Old Ross in the late thirteenth century the wages of 4 binders, 1 reaper, 4 shepherds, 1 cowherd, 1 watchman, 1 waggoner and 1 janitor for half a year came to 26s. There was also 1 dairyman and 1 calf keeper regularly employed with the others. But there were also casual labourers employed for special jobs, such as the man 'hired to make holes in the shingles (4,000 of them) for 15 days and to carry them to the roof of the grange' at 1½d. a day. Labour, then, was a major cost factor on any manor, despite the existence of labour services.

The lay-out of the manor

Only the largest manors would have stone castles, such as those at Carlow, Nenagh and Trim. The smaller manors had less pretentious hall dwelling, each with its own particular scattering of outhouses. The lay-out at Cloncurry was probably quite typical. The 1304 extent describes 'a courtyard, the walls of which are broken and in which there is a hall with a roof of straw and one division of which is in ruins, and also a small dilapidated dwelling and a motte on which is situated a one roomed building with a wooden roof'. There was a garden and a farmyard 'with broken walls in which there are two small eight-post barns and one grain kiln badly roofed and one small house in which is laid a threshing board but which is not a barn nor a grain store'. Beside the gate of the yard was a cow byre. There was also, of course, a haggard and a dovecot.

At Duleek, which was a monastic grange, there was a more elaborate series of buildings arranged around a courtyard. On the east side there was a chapel, a hall with a thatched kitchen and dairy, a stable, a long room (with a closet adjoining), another room called 'the knight's chamber', all roofed with tiles. There was also a cellar under the long room, which was used as a pantry for bread and ale. Similarly, there was a larder under the knight's room, and a stable at the end of the long room. On the south side of the court was a bakery and a brew-house (which had a loft for keeping the malt). There was a kiln and an oven, a small granary, a small pigsty, and a long, thatched byre. On the north side was a sheep pen and a thatched stable. Then came the 'high gate', a great stone building, with two rooms for guests and the gate-keeper's room. Between the gate and the kitchen was a walled garden, and another walled garden lay to the east of the chapel. The haggard lay along the west side of the courtyard, with only one thatched building on that side (the 'kilnehous'). In the haggard was the usual dovecot and there was another in the meadow which also contained the water-mill.

The only significant development in manorial lay-out in the later middle ages was the appearance of the tower house, an easily defended residence. With the gradual growth of disorder, especially in areas not within easy reach of Dublin, it became necessary for the manorial lords to be far more defence conscious than had been the case in more settled times. Tower houses provided a simple, if expensive, answer. There had been a need for defence in some areas in an earlier period and to this day there is the physical evidence of moated sites (usually rectangular earthworks) which were the defended homes of Anglo-Norman tenants. The Old Ross accounts for 1283–4 contain a record of expenditure on digging and barricading such a defended site at Balliconnor in county Wexford.

The main expense was the construction of the elaborate fence after the great ditch was dug. For example, it took 660 stakes, cut in the wood at a cost of 19½d., to hold the fence. The wages of the different carpenters (including one Irishman, Gregory O Morrough) employed at different stages in the work accounted for most of the expenditure.

Agriculture

Part of each manor was reserved for the lord in demesne. At Cloncurry in 1304 there was just over 125 acres in demesne. Of this 34 acres lay fallow, 43 acres were sown with wheat and 48 with oats. The extent recorded that 'it is necessary to plough three times for wheat and once for oats and the cost of tilling an acre in any season is 8 pence and the cost of harrowing an acre whether for wheat or oats is 3 pence. A one-horse harrow will harrow half an acre per day'. A plough of 8 oxen 'properly attended' will plough 25 acres in a season. There was also 11½ acres kept in meadow. Mowing cost 5d. an acre. 'and the shaking out and gathering in the meadow' cost 4d.

The yield was low. At Cloncurry it was stated that 'an acre of wheat will yield 2½ crannocks in an ordinary year and an acre of oats 2 crannocks'. To sow an acre of wheat took 5 bushels. This seems fairly typical. At Drogheda in 1297, 22 acres of wheat produced 40 crannocks; at Kildare in 1305, 6 acres produced 12 crannocks. The cost, too, was high. As labour grew scarcer, partly the result of emigration and the spectacular fall in numbers after the Black Death, wages naturally had to rise. We have already seen the vain attempt to peg wages in 1299, showing that a problem already existed before the end of the thirteenth century. Equipment, too, was very expensive and had to be regularly replaced. Even fertilisation, primitive and inefficient as it was, meant a huge outlay. In 1288, for example, each barge load of sand cost 5d. at Old Ross. The cost of sanding an acre seemed to vary: at Kilcoleman it was 5s.;

at Old Ross 8s.; at Cumban 4s. The sand was taken from the tidal estuary of the Barrow and the cost per acre was largely determined by the carriage. Burning the land – which was a method the Anglo-Normans acquired from the Irish – was cheaper, but less efficient. It cost 16d. an acre, plus an extra 3 or 4d. an acre to spread the ashes. Altogether, then, agriculture was a costly business, where the margin of profit was small. In the later middle ages, when the state of Ireland became increasingly more disturbed, it is hardly surprising that tillage declined and that the traditional Irish emphasis on the pastoral reasserted itself.

While the demesne lands were usually in a block, the lands of the tenants were scattered in the great, open fields which made up most of the manor, though there is evidence that in the later middle ages holdings were being consolidated. Typically, however, the tenant held strips in different fields, taking his share of bad land with the good. In 1477, for example, an owner at Rathcoole in county Dublin had 26 acres of arable land, scattered in twenty parcels, and one acre of meadow in four. By the fifteenth century in the eastern part of Ireland there is evidence of increasing enclosure; but before that, enclosure was rare and strip cultivation was the norm.

There was a three course rotation of crops; winter corn, spring corn and fallow. Oats was the largest crop, with wheat, barley (which was grown for brewing, supplemented by oat malt) and rye following. Garden cultivation was also common. On some manors, as we saw, there were walled gardens. But more commonly gardens were fenced with thorns. Root crops were practically unknown, but beans, peas and onions were grown. Leeks, apples and herbs were produced in the garden at Old Ross. And in 1283 the same manor produced 231 stone of cheese which was sold at 8d. a stone.

Perhaps the most valuable asset on most manors was the stock. At Old Ross in 1280 there were 505 sheep and 313 lambs – sales in the same year accounted for 221 sheep and 42 lambs. The great value of sheep can clearly be seen from the sharp increase in numbers from the 818 accounted for in 1280. By 1284 it had climbed to nearly 1,400, and by 1288 it had reached 2,160. It is evident that the economy of the manor was dependent more on sheep than on anything else. In 1284, for example, the account listed the following stock: 7 afers (a farm horse), 39 oxen (of which 2 died and 7 were sold), 1 bull, 29 cows (of which 2 died and 2 were sold), 1 yearling, 14 heifers and 27 calves (of which 6 died). Pigs were only occasionally kept; but there were 9 swans in 1283 and 11 peacocks.

The value of the sheep was partly the mutton, partly the milk of ewes (which was used to make cheese), and in part their utility in manuring the land. But above all it was their wool, the 'golden fleece' of the middle ages, which made them the most valuable animals on any manor. In the thirteenth century the Italian merchants in particular sought Irish wool as an addition to the finer English wool and caused the export trade in wool to boom.

Trade and commercial life
Wool was increasingly in demand as the great cloth industries of Flanders and Italy expanded at that time. There is no doubt that it was the most important single item of Ireland's export trade until it declined in the later middle ages. In 1273, for example, and again in 1300 Irish wool was taxed in Bruges. Flemish merchants were well established here in the thirteenth century and were to be found all over the land of peace. But it was the Italians, and especially the great companies from Lucca and Florence (such as the Ricardi, the Bardi and above all the Frescobaldi) who dominated the wool trade and who, indeed, made a massive investment of capital in Ireland on which the prosperity of the thirteenth century was based.

The real significance of the wool trade is demonstrated

by the surviving customs accounts. In 1275 a custom was imposed on all exports of wool and hides, limiting export to a fixed number of ports spread fairly evenly around the coast. From then on the custom brought in an average of about £1,400 a year to the Dublin exchequer (at a time when its total income was just over £6,000 a year on average). The little port of Dingle, for example, provided just over £15 in 1287, nearly £5 in 1288, £10 in 1290, and over £14 in 1292. Such small sums may look ridiculous now; but they represent a huge export of wool and hides from such a remote part of Ireland. In sacks of wool (each sack weighing 42 stone) the figures would represent 45 sacks (or 1,880 stone), 15 (or 630 stone), 30 (or 1,260 stone), and 42 (or 1,764 stone). In hides the same sums would represent 4,500; 1,500; 3,000; and 4,200.

There was a gradual decline in custom revenue in the latter part of the reign of Edward I, until it was less than half what it had been. The decline continued in the fourteenth century. There seems to have been no recovery and at the end of the century the Irish council complained that the custom revenue 'used to be a great part of the substance of the revenue there and now little comes to the king'. But this does not necessarily mean a decline in trade. For one thing, much more of the customs revenue was spent locally and never reached the exchequer. Also, the disturbed conditions often made the collection of custom impossible, without preventing ships leaving non-custom ports. All the evidence suggests that in the later middle ages there was a substantial export trade in wool, though now mainly to England. The coarse Irish wool was ideal for making heavy cloth and Irish cloaks were exported to many countries. It is clear that in the fourteenth century the woollen industry made great strides in Ireland. Skilled weavers migrated to England and found ready employment in the rapidly expanding English cloth industry, especially in the west country. Worsted, serge, frieze, as well as ready-made cloaks, were exported in the later middle ages and may have caused a decline in the export of raw wool. Linen was another Irish cloth which was much in demand. In one year more than 20,000 yards of linen were imported by Bristol alone.

Hides were probably a more important commodity in Ireland's export trade than wool or woollen cloths. Europe rather than England provided the main market, and there is evidence of astonishing quantities of Irish hides being imported by the great leather industries of Pisa: nearly 34,000 in half a year (1466–67) and over 24,000 in another half-year (1482–83). Thousands more were shipped to Flanders annually and some to France. Other skins and furs were regularly exported, a luxury trade which brought a high margin of profit. A certain amount of wheat and other cereals was also shipped, though this tended to fluctuate wildly since famine was a regular occurrence. Indeed one reason for the swing towards the pastoral was not only the high profit to be made from cattle and the smaller risk they offered in dangerous times, but also because cattle were safer since they were less at the mercy of the vagaries of the weather than crops. By the fifteenth century Ireland was regularly importing corn, especially from Bristol. By then fish had become a major export, mainly through Bristol, where a well-known proverb said: 'Herring of Sligo and salmon of Bann, has made in Bristol many a rich man'. It is impossible to quantify this trade, but vast numbers were sent to England. Some meat was also regularly exported. Hawks were always in demand, as were Irish horses. Timber, lard, tallow, wax, and the occasional manufactured article were other items of trade.

Salt and iron were two items which Ireland had to import; wine was another, as well as a huge variety of goods which were not manufactured in Ireland. Beer, too, was brought from England. Much more important, however, was the expensive English cloth which was bought, mainly through Bristol. Nevertheless, it seems that in the later middle ages the balance of trade was heavily in Ireland's favour. Families grew rich on the great exports, since most of the trade was kept in local hands. Towns like Galway in the fifteenth century could show physical evidence of the wealth of some, at least, of the citizens. There was, then, a demand for luxuries and it was readily met. Spices of all kinds, silk, jewels, precious ornaments, and rich cloths were brought in regularly. The murage grants (customs on specified articles entering the town) of most towns show an astonishing variety of luxuries available. Dublin in 1336 was levying tolls on such items as silk, cloth of gold, satin, diaper, cloth from Flanders, Normandy and Brabant, linen from France, figs, raisins, spices, in addition to a huge list of manufactured goods.

There was, of course, a flourishing internal trade as well. One result of the Anglo-Norman invasion was that towns and markets sprang up everywhere. Roads were built, rivers cleared for better communication, passes cut in the woods, bridges constructed and ferries established. Royal mints provided a regular series of acceptable coins. All of this made for a commercial revolution in Ireland. It is true that in the later middle ages many of the centres of trade disappeared. A falling population, caused partly by the continuing plague, partly by emigration, and to some extent too the result of the frequent wars which were a great scourge in many parts of the country, meant a decline in commercial activity. But there is plenty of evidence that commercial life was still healthy and that, if anything, the country grew more prosperous in the fifteenth century.

The towns

While the country producer naturally benefited from the rich returns from trade, it was in the towns that there was the greatest concentration of wealth. The vast majority of these were of Anglo-Norman origin and certainly their institutions were all derived from charters of the king or of some great lord. Many of them had grown up around a castle, at the centre of a lordship or at some point favourable for trade. Others were on the coast and derived their main wealth from trade through the port. Most were walled in the later middle ages, being granted tolls (murage) to meet the cost of building. They had the right of self-government, their own courts, and usually the right to hold fairs and markets. Many of them were hardly more than villages and can hardly have provided the inhabitants with many of the comforts of life. But the larger ones had many amenities to offer, with paved and occasionally lighted streets, shops and tradesmen of all sorts, even running water. Galway even went so far in the fifteenth century as to replace the common law with 'the law of the Emperor called the Civil Law' (as reported in parliament in 1476). This was Roman law and it probably came into use as a result of Galway's far-flung trading connexions with many parts of Europe, where this law was respected.

The right of the chartered towns to manage their own affairs was a vital factor in their development as trading centres. The power of legislation enabled them to make bye-laws regulating commercial activity, to the advantage of the citizens naturally. But it also provided the security and proper conditions which would attract outside traders to the town. Apart from that, municipalities were able to provide for the comfort and safety of the inhabitants by regular legislation. A set of ordinances of the common council of the city of Dublin prescribed different fines and punishments for a whole series of offences. It fixed prices – 'for a good goose, 2 pence; for 2 good rabbits, 3 pence; for 2 middle-sized rabbits, 1 penny' and so on. Regulations for the sale of different commodities were announced. Rates of wages were firmly fixed – 'for weaving cloth 30 ells in length, 3 shillings; for dying thirty ells of cloth, 3 pence per ell'. Where houses were mainly of wood, with thatched roofs, and were clustered together in narrow streets, fire was always a terrible hazard. This is reflected in a Dublin ordinance, which fixed the fines to be levied on a householder who was responsible for a fire. 'Any person answerable for the burning of a street shall be arrested, cast into the middle of the fire, or pay 100 shillings'. The problems of sanitation were immense, and keeping the streets reasonably clean was obviously of great importance. In Dublin it was enacted that 'every householder must cleanse the portion of the street before his own door, under penalty of 12 pence'. Pigs were a huge problem, impossible to control and often running wild in the streets. A letter of 1489 gives a grim picture of Dublin: 'The king has been informed that dungheaps, swine, pigsties and other nuisances in the streets, lanes and suburbs of Dublin infect the air and produce mortality, fevers and pestilence throughout that city. Many citizens and sojourners have thus died in Dublin. The fear of pestilence prevents the coming thither of lords, ecclesiastics and lawyers. Great detriments thence arise to his majesty, as well as dangers to his subjects and impediments to business. The king commands the mayor and bailiffs to cause forthwith the removal of all swine, and to have the streets and lands freed from ordure, so as to prevent loss of life from pestilential exhalations. The mayor is to expel all Irish vagrants and mendicants from the city'.

Fear of the plague was ever-present and the belief that disease was bred by filth and decaying flesh led to frequent attempts to control the slaughter of animals and the disposal of bodies. In Kilkenny in October 1337, it was decreed that 'if anyone be found washing clothing or the intestines of animals or anything else in the fountains of the said town they shall be forfeited and if anyone be found committing any other enormity in the said fountains he shall be put in the tumbrel'. Like Dublin, Kilkenny too compelled each householder to 'cleanse the pavement against his house and this twice a week, that is on Wednesday and Saturday'. But all efforts to keep the cities clean were defeated. Dublin in 1459 had to issue an ordinance that 'every fisher that hath a board in the fishambles and casteth guts under their boards and wash not their boards after they hath done their market, that they shall pay a groat as often times as they found guilty thereof'.

One of the biggest nuisances of all was the beggars and vagrants who swarmed through the towns. Dublin in 1455 ordained 'that no manner of beggar dwelling within the said city nor scholar walk by night at all abegging, upon the pain of forfeiting of what may be found with them'. But the main reason for fearing vagrants was that they were carriers of the plague. The oath taken by the provost of Dublin had him promise 'to banish all beggars in time of sickness and plague'.

One of the most famous ordinances of Dublin concerned the pageants of Corpus Christi, an old set of regulations which were confirmed in 1498. Many 'pilgrims' were attracted to Dublin by the great processions held on the feasts of Corpus Christi, St George and St Patrick. In association with Corpus Christi, which was adopted by the trade gilds as their principal festival, a linked series or cycle of religious plays was performed by the gilds. Plays were performed at other times of the year. In 1528, for example, the earl of Ossory, then chief governor, was invited to a different play every day during Christmas. The stage was set up on Hoggen Green (now College Green) and on it different trade gilds acted plays appropriate to their craft: the vintners told the story of Bacchus; the carpenters dealt with Joseph and Mary; the smiths with Vulcan, and so on. But it was the Corpus Christi plays which were by far the most numerous, miscellaneous, and imposing. According to the regulations, they began with the story of Adam and Eve, performed by the glovers; then Cain and Abel, by the shoemakers; Noah, by the mariners, ship-carpenters and salmon-takers; Abraham and Isaac, by the weavers.

Altogether there seem to have been fourteen plays (or 'pageants'), each in the hands of an appropriate gild. Thus, the butchers were to be 'tormentors, with their garments well and clearly painted'; the fishermen, apostles; the skinners were to provide a camel, the painters were to paint it, the porters were to carry it. Fines were specified for default, though it seems likely that the competitive spirit among the gilds would keep them up to scratch.

These gilds had originated in the Merchant Gild, which included all who were involved in trade. But by the later middle ages the huge numbers engaged in a wide variety of trades and crafts made diversification necessary and a large number of separate gilds was formed. These regulated the particular craft or trade, set standards, controlled admission (usually excluding Gaelic Irish, a practice roundly condemned in 1355 by the famous archbishop of Armagh, Richard fitz Ralph), set the terms of apprenticeship, normally seven years, and the qualifications demanded of masters. Each gild had its own patron saint, whose festival was celebrated with a mass and a feast. Each was attached to a church or a chapel in a large church.

The members of the gilds were usually well to do, owning property and chattels of value. When John Hammond, a cobbler, died in 1383, he owned various pieces of silver, valuable utensils and acres of wheat, barley, oats and hay, as well as a large quantity of leather and a stock of '19 dozen and 4 of shoes, each dozen worth 3 shillings'. An enormous list of debts was owing to him by customers. 'The prior of Holy Trinity owes, for 1 pair of boots, 2s.; for the making of 1 pair of boots, 8d.; for 8 pairs of shoes, 3s. 4d.; for 33 pairs of shoes, 5s. 9d.'. He had some well-known people as customers (such as the prior of Kilmainham), so he was clearly an important cobbler. In his will, as well as the usual money for masses and for candles, he left bequests to a number of churches. He also left 20s. 'for wine, spices, and other expenses at his burial'. Provision of food and drink for the wake was a common feature of such wills as have survived from the towns.

People like Hammond must have enjoyed a fair standard of living. At a higher social level we can get a very vivid impression of daily life from the surviving household accounts of the prior of Holy Trinity, Dublin. His apartments certainly were not sumptuously furnished, since the floors were bare, the chairs and seats seem to have been made on the spot ('in hire of a certain man making straw chairs, seats, and straw stools for the prior's chamber at Dublin'), the table-ware was pewter and valuable enough to employ a goldsmith to mark them. This was in marked contrast to the priory at Kells, where a kitchen account of 1282 shows 22d. being spent on wooden vessels for the table. There is no sign of silver at either place. There is one payment (6d. 'also given to Ymna the washerwoman, for the washing of linen cloths of the prior's chamber for the term of Easter') which suggests that table-linen may possibly have been used.

If there is an ascetic touch about the furnishings, there is certainly nothing austere about the quality of the meals. Three were served every day: breakfast (an innovation in a religious household), dinner at about noon, and supper. Only on Friday was there abstinence from meat. At breakfast, which was usually a substantial meal, bread and wine or ale, were regularly served, and occasionally oysters, salmon, capons or pasties. The other two meals were always substantial. There was plenty of meat and fowl: beef, mutton, lamb (served as early as 11 February), pork, rabbits, capons, geese, larks, pigeons, plovers and goslings. In Lent, and on Fridays, plenty of fish was available: salmon, oysters, salted fish and herrings were the most common; less rarely, for special guests, trout, eels, turbot, plaice, gurnard and salted eels were on the menu. Bread, of course, and wine (white as well as red) and ale were always available, with butter and cheese. Onions seem to have

19

been the only vegetable used – the beans and peas which were grown in the garden were mainly used for fodder or consumed by labourers. Imported produce included olive oil (in regular use), almonds, walnuts, rice, salt, pepper, verjuice, figs, mustard, saffron and spices. Surprisingly, considering the amount of apples grown, fruit was very scarce. Pears appear only once, when the archbishop was entertained. Piment, a drink made with wine, honey and various spices, was sometimes bought.

The priory was situated close by Winetavern Street, the street of taverns and wine shops, and so was able to buy wine in bulk. More surprisingly, the prior often bought ready-cooked food from the 'Vicus Cocorum', the modern Cook Street. Providing good fare in an emergency, then, was not difficult. When the sheriff of the county and other guests turned up for dinner on 12 February 1338, they were given wine (9d.), 5 pasties of fowl baked (9½d.). And when they remained for supper they got wine (6d.), 2 roast chickens and other fowl bought (4d.), half a lamb (2d.) and roast beef (4d.). Even though no meat was eaten in Lent, there was an abundance of other good things. An elaborate meal was provided on Ash Wednesday, which included herrings, white fish, salmon, ginger, mustard, almonds and rice. The latter combination was regular and frequent, suggesting that a later belief in the nutritious value of almonds and rice cooked together was already prevalent in fourteenth-century Ireland.

The clothes worn by the prior were very much what would have been worn by a layman of the same class. He usually wore a tunic of wool, with a surcoat over (or the longer capa) with a hood, each of which was plentifully furred. He wore gloves as well, and shoes or boots. He rode his own palfrey, with its own special groom. His household varied considerably, especially the squires and clerks. But he always had a chamberlain (or housekeeper), a cook, and some personal servants. Doubtless a great magnate would have had a much larger household; but the prior's must have been typical of many lesser people.

Leisure and entertainment

There is no mention in these accounts of entertainment being provided for the guests, though it is a striking fact that what may be the oldest English morality play (called *The Pride of Life* by its editor) was hurriedly jotted down on the blank dorse of one membrane. Probably in the possession of some guest, the making of a copy suggests a keen interest in such writings. Outside the priory there is plenty of evidence that in the great households entertainment was provided by minstrels, harpers, 'rhymers', and troubadours (often Gaelic). Giraldus had remarked on the Gaelic flair for music: 'they seem to me to be incomparably more skilled in these (i.e. musical instruments) then any other people that I have seen'. Music certainly played a large part in the lives of the people everywhere. In Kilkenny in the fourteenth century, Bishop Ledrede of Ossory was so scandalised by the secular ballads of the day that he composed sixty songs in Latin, using popular airs, which were intended to edify. But the people went on singing the English songs, though only three later ones survive from Kilkenny, one of which begins: 'Graceful and gay, on her is set all my thought. Unless she have pity on me today she will bring me to death'. In Armagh, a provincial council in the late fourteenth century renewed old prohibitions against 'mimes, jugglers, poets, drummers or harpers'. The recently discovered early fifteenth-century inscribed slates from Smarmore, county Louth, which are largely the work of the local schoolmaster (who also acted as doctor and veterinary surgeon for the village), contain musical notations which are polyphonic, not plainsong, probably current dance-tunes.

Among the decrees of the provincial council of Armagh just mentioned was one which forbade the game of *galbardy* (which some historians have presumed to be hurling) because 'mortal sins and beating and often homicides are committed'. The famous statutes of Kilkenny of 1366 also outlawed in the march 'the games which men call hurlings with great clubs at ball upon the ground, from which great evils and maims have arisen to the weakening of the defence of the said land'. It also forbade 'coitings' (throwing quoits?) and recommended archery, throwing lances 'and other gentle games which appertain to arms'. The context makes it quite clear that these were games played among the Anglo- Irish. Jousting, too, was popular, as was hunting. One of the few surviving fragments of a wall painting from medieval Ireland in Abbeyknockmoy in county Galway, shows a hunting scene. A Dublin provincial council of 1367 forbade the holding of dances, wrestling matches or other improper games in cemeteries. Church-yards were a convenient centre for popular games of all sorts. But the wrestling matches which were popular were usually held in a field. As is often the case with competitive sport, particularly between towns or parishes, violence could easily break out. In 1305 at a wrestling contest at Naas, for which a prize was offered, a quarrel developed. One man shot an arrow at another, and a third was struck with a hatchet. At a time when most free men carried weapons, a quarrel could all too easily lead to serious injury. It was usually the custom, therefore, to lay weapons aside during a friendly sporting contest – as had indeed been agreed in the case just mentioned. The contest was between 'the country men of the barony of Naas and the men of the town of Naas' and it was agreed beforehand that 'none of them should come armed, lest hurt should happen'. The townsmen broke the agreement and, as we saw, hurt did happen. A spleen remained between the two sides, 'on account of which', a justiciar's court was told, 'the peace in the parts of Naas is much diminished and divers ills have happened'.

Time hardly seemed to exist in those days when clocks were few. Men measured time naturally, from dawn to dusk, with noon as a half-way mark. The natural seasons, the time of sowing and of harvesting, were the times to be remembered. Another great way of keeping track of time was by using the saints' days. There were so many of these scattered throughout the year that they provided regular points of reference. They were the more easily remembered since they were not working days. It has been estimated that in Europe there were so many feast-days in the later middle ages that on average there were only 200 working days in the year. In Ireland there is evidence that the increase in the number of saints' days was creating a problem. The fifth decree of the provincial council held by Archbishop Minot of Dublin referred to this: 'Since experience and actual fact make it plain that the multiplication of feast beyond what is customary hinders work in the fields and in the city, which is most necessary for both clergy and laity and for the common people, especially the poor who through poverty are unable to till their little plots of land and are prevented from receiving the charitable help of wealthier neighbours . . . yet in fact they (the feasts) provide cause of sin to those workmen, many of whom never or rarely enter their parish church at hours when masses are celebrated, but spend almost all the feast-day or at least the greater part thereof in taverns and drunkenness and other illicit acts of pleasure'. The multiplicity of feasts created a leisure problem which was only partly solved by the available recreational facilities. The archbishop was certainly right in drawing attention to the taverns.

Then, as now, many spent their leisure time in taverns, where food as well as drink was normally available. Oysters, in particular, seem to have been a frequent accompaniment to the wine and ale which was sold. One problem, at a time when the smallest coin in circulation was vastly in excess of the prices charged for the normal measures of food and drink, was how to pay. One must suppose that with regular customers bills were run up. But there is proof that tokens were employed, of the kind found (more than 2,000 of them) in the excavations at Winetavern Street.

Much violence was associated with taverns and drinking. Quarrels could break out over trivialities. A man was killed in Drogheda in 1310 after such a quarrel. He was Jordan, the chaplain of Hugh de Lacy, who with others of Hugh's household went to drink at the inn of Michael of Trim. They were found there by a tailor, Robert le Lumynour, who inquired if Jordan wished to have cloaks made. Jordan said not, but that in any case he would have them made by some other tailor in Drogheda better than Robert. They came to blows and after being separated those in the tavern made Jordan and his men get on their horses and made Robert go home by a different route. But one of Jordan's men rode after Robert and attacked him with his sword. Robert took a big club from a servant nearby and defended himself. He was then attacked by another swordsman from the entourage of Jordan, but he managed to drive him off ('in terror', according to the court record). Robert then went into the attack and followed the pair, but not being able to get at the swordsmen 'he struck Jordan with the club on the back of the neck, so that he fell to the ground and soon afterwards died'.

One of the most extraordinary cases to come before the justiciar's court in 1307, concerned the priory of St Peter in Trim. Some of the brothers there 'feeling themselves too much restrained by the prior armed themselves secretly with swords and other arms for the purpose of doing mischief'. On the Feast of SS Peter and Paul, they assembled in the evening 'complaining that they were so restrained by the prior that they could not have drink at their will, as they were accustomed to have'. They tried to have their way by force, brutally killing one brother on their way to the cellar. Another was killed there, struck by one of the malcontents 'with a sword on the neck so that he nearly cut off his head'. Then they forced the door and had access to the drink.

This is an extreme (though not unique) example of even religious houses being plagued by the problem of excessive drinking in the later middle ages. It is evident that, as ecclesiastics complained, it created a grave social problem. In an age where violence was endemic, it complicated an already impossible situation for the government. For the end of the thirteenth century saw a gradual increase in the incidence of crime, more frequent outbreaks of war, an upsurging of violence that threatened the rule of law. Thereafter the government found itself ceasing to be able to cope and had to restrict the scope and the scale of its activity. The institutions of government were found to be inadequate and the governance of Ireland suffered as a result.

County and liberty boundaries

LOUTH = Names of counties and liberties

Counties and liberties

2 The Governance of Medieval Ireland

ALL over the feudal world kings were faced with the same problem of how best to govern their subjects and maintain their own rights. In more primitive times, when the area ruled was small and the king was able to perambulate easily, personal rule was possible. The king regularly showed himself to his people and held his court, dispensed justice, inflicted punishments, exacted payments, made rewards and grants. He even led them to war in person. But with the expansion of kingdoms, the king had to learn how to govern at a distance. He had therefore to develop a system of administration which would enable him to perform his regular functions from afar and through intermediaries. Only in this way could he exercise control over his subjects and protect them in their rights.

In the case of Ireland, such control from a distance was even more important. It was essential for the English government to exercise authority over the colony as it developed. At the same time the colonial government itself had to be able to maintain the rule of law throughout the lordship in places far removed from Dublin. There was therefore a double problem, involving two levels of control: that of the king over his Dublin government, and that of Dublin over the lordship. It is important to understand this, for part of the problem of Ireland in the later middle ages was the partial (and at times complete) breakdown of these controls. Powerful Anglo-Irish gained an ascendancy which made them less and less amenable to control.

By the time of the Anglo-Norman invasion of Ireland a sophisticated system of government had been developed in England. This, with modifications, was imported into Ireland and through it the king, as lord of Ireland, governed his lordship. Because he was so frequently out of England, the office of justiciar was developed to take the place of the king and govern on his behalf. This office was naturally introduced into Ireland. The titles of the earliest chief governors varied, but from the time of John de Courcy in 1185, the title of justiciar (*justiciarius*) was regularly employed. Early in the fourteenth century a lieutenant was first appointed and this was the title regularly employed from the end of that century. The old title of justiciar was henceforth normally reserved for a chief governor elected in Ireland during an emergency vacancy of that office. If, as often happened in the fifteenth century, the lieutenant was a person of such high standing in England that he never came to Ireland, he acted through a deputy.

The chief governor was head of the government. He was the supreme judge (a function he ceased to perform after the emergence of the justiciar's bench with its own chief justice), commander-in-chief of the armed forces of the colony and the chief executive in the civil service. He normally had the right to issue pardons, to appoint or dismiss royal officials (an exception was usually made of the more important offices, such as that of chancellor and treasurer, since these were automatically members of the council and therefore a check on the actions of the chief governor – though control of even those offices fell into the hands of the earls of Kildare in the fifteenth century), and generally to exercise many of the prerogatives reserved to the king. The chief governor, acting of course with the advice of the council, declared war and made peace, received submissions, summoned those owing military service. He himself had his own armed retinue, the nucleus of any army sent on campaign. At first, when the justiciar's salary was fixed at £500 a year, this retinue consisted of only twenty men at arms (including himself); but in the later middle ages the chief governor was normally appointed under contract for a fixed term of office and with an agreed stipend which was very much larger than the traditional £500 and for which he had to provide a much larger force of men at arms and archers. The governor, too, exercised the royal right of purveyance, which enabled him to seize food, goods and transport for his household and for war, though the full market price was supposed to be paid to the owners.

The council

It was the chief governor who had the sole right, delegated to him by the king, to summon the parliaments and councils through which he governed. The council was in origin derived from the feudal obligation where every tenant had to give counsel to his lord. With the feudal settlement of Ireland such a council naturally emerged. At first it met infrequently, attended by different magnates whose advice might be especially valuable, or who might conveniently be at hand. But during the thirteenth century, when the business of government became increasingly complex, more frequent council meetings became necessary. Gradually a privy or secret council (*secretum concilium*) emerged, consisting in the main of the chief ministers of the Crown who could normally be expected to be available to the justiciar, together with others who were specially appointed as councillors. By the early fourteenth century such a council is well established and its ministerial character well defined. The councillors all took oaths not to reveal the secret business of the council and those who were not ministers received a fee. In 1320 there were present at a council meeting the justiciar, chancellor, treasurer, escheator, two justices of the justiciar's bench, two barons of the exchequer and a number of non-official members. It is clear that gradually the ministerial element predominated, so that the non-ministers took little or no part in the routine business of the council. In the fifteenth century this inner group numbered seven and consisted mainly of lawyers: the chancellor, the treasurer, the two chief justices, the chief baron of the exchequer, the master of the rolls and the king's serjeant-at-law. Others might occasionally attend, but they had ceased to be regular members. We shall see how important this development was to be in enabling the Kildares to retain control over the Irish government in the later fifteenth century.

It was the council which normally advised the chief governor in matters of policy as well as in the day to day business of government. The patents by which lieutenants and justiciars were appointed usually insisted that they were to act 'by the advice of our council in the land of Ireland' and it was before the council that they normally were sworn in office. The council, in fact, was the king's council in Ireland and acted as a check on the chief governor there. Normally, of course, they worked in close cooperation. But if such cooperation broke down, as it occasionally did, government was made nearly impossible. Some chief governors quarrelled with different ministers and thus failed to secure the cooperation of the council. The fourth earl of Ormond met with opposition from a number of chancellors and treasurers in the first half of the fifteenth century. Lord Grey, in 1478, found the chancellor violently opposed to him, refusing to seal messages on his behalf. Sir John Sutton, in 1428, drove the treasurer out of Ireland. Thomas Butler, prior of Kilmainham, met with vigorous opposition from the council in 1409, when he was deputy for Thomas of Lancaster. But opposition of this kind was exceptional and governor and council nearly always worked in the greatest harmony.

Close contact was maintained with the English government, through messengers who, if they were of ministerial rank, frequently attended sessions of the council and helped to maintain close links with the king. Even in the later middle ages, when Anglo-Irish separatism had allowed the chief governor to gain a dangerous measure of control over the council, messages and instructions continued to flow across the Irish sea. By then the council had succeeded in impressing its views on parliament, which had begun to develop an authority of its own. It was felt, therefore, that messages which came from parliament as distinct from the council would carry greater authority in England and so this became the normal practice, even though council still sent messages of its own. Parliament had become an instrument of government.

Parliament

The origins of parliament in Ireland are obscure and it was slow to assume the form which it possessed at the end of the middle ages. But there seems little doubt that it began as an afforced, or enlarged, meeting of the council when there was especially difficult business to be discussed and far-reaching decisions to be taken. In other words, the council remained the core or nucleus of any parliament subsequently. The existence of such an assembly from early in the thirteenth century naturally made it easy for ministers to refer particularly thorny problems to it. It became a judicial as well as a consultative and legislative assembly and it retained its judicial character right to the end of our period. By the end of the thirteenth century, too, communities as well as individuals were presenting petitions to parliament seeking redress for grievances. Much legislation was derived from such petitions and by the later middle ages it was normal for parliamentary enactments to be initiated by petitions presented by the commons, after they had deliberated apart. From the mid-fifteenth century most of these petitions were written as separate bills and the resulting acts were enrolled on the rolls of parliament. It should be said, however, that much of the resulting legislation was trivial and ephemeral, intended to deal with immediate (and often personal) problems. Even the famous Poynings' Law of 1495, which effectively ended the independence of the medieval Irish parliament by making it compulsory for all bills to be first approved by the king and his council in England, only became permanent because it suited later generations. Very little Irish legislation assumed the importance or the permanence of the Statutes of Kilkenny of 1366.

The first Irish parliament we know of met in Castledermot in 1264. It developed rapidly thereafter, following the English pattern, though because of different circumstances in Ireland important differences arose. For one thing, the Irish lower clergy (together with the spiritual peers – the bishops and the greater abbots) continued to be represented in parliament through clerical proctors, forming a third 'house' of their own until the reformation. The lower clergy were not summoned to a parliament until 1370, but it is likely that they were represented in parliaments during the previous decade. Before that they were represented by their bishops, just as the 'commons' (the local communities of shires, liberties and towns) had been represented by the magnates. It was only very gradually that the commons came to parliament. They were first summoned in the late thirteenth century and increasingly in the fourteenth century to discuss taxation. But it was not until the last quarter of the fourteenth century that they succeeded in establishing themselves as an integral part of parliament. This was because the principle of the parliamentary subsidy was accepted in late fourteenth-century Ireland – that is that general taxation was now a matter solely for parliament in which taxation was discussed. It was an easy transition from this to the doctrine that the commons were entitled to be present in any parliament and it is interesting to note that in the earliest surviving rolls of parliament from the fifteenth century, where the authority of parliament is quoted in justification of the different acts, the formula employed always includes the commons.

It must not be thought that once the commons had established themselves in the Irish parliament that it became in any way democratic as a result. Those who held the franchise were drawn exclusively from the wealthier class in town and country and those whom they elected were equally drawn from a narrow class – the knights of the countryside and the burgesses of the town. In addition, the area of Ireland which was represented tended to shrink all the time. Not until the reign of Henry VIII was Gaelic Ireland represented when certain Gaelic lords were raised to the ranks of the peerage. By the early fifteenth century only eleven counties and ten towns were sending representatives, which meant a total of only forty-four in the commons (since each constituency returned two representatives, two knights from the shires and two burgesses from the towns). Only the area covered by counties Dublin, Kildare, Louth and Meath were regularly represented, with the town of Waterford. Other communities might send representatives, but only occasionally.

This same regional character of the fifteenth-century parliament is reflected in the clerical representation as well. The dioceses of the Dublin metropolitan province were fairly regularly represented, as were those of Cashel; but from the province of Armagh only Armagh itself and Meath ever sent representatives, while none came from the western province of Tuam. The attendance of heads of religious houses was equally regional. In 1375 nine Cistercian abbots (of Baltinglass; St Mary's, Dublin; Dunbrody; Duiske; Jerpoint; Mellifont; Monaster Nenagh; Tintern; and Tracton, county Cork) and six heads of houses of canons regular (St Thomas, Holy Trinity and All Hallows, Dublin; Connell, Kildare; Kells and St Peter's Trim,

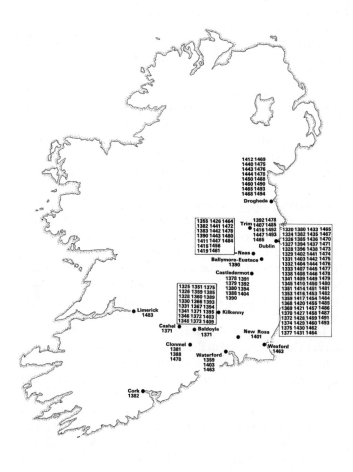

Parliaments and Councils, 1320–1494

Meath) were summoned. But by the fifteenth century the list had shrunk to only six – the abbots of Mellifont, St Mary's and Baltinglass, the priors of Connell and Trim and the prior of Kilmainham (who was regularly acting as a minister of the Crown).

Only a small number of spiritual peers, therefore, sat in the upper house with the temporal peers. The number of the latter, too, continued to shrink and to display the same regional character. It was not until late in the fourteenth century that the number of peers, or those who had the right to be summoned to parliament, was defined. It is important to realise that up to then attendance at parliament was a burden and duty, not a privilege to be eagerly sought. Those magnates who received individual summonses to parliament had an obligation to attend – they were fined for absence. The number varied, since there seemed to be no easy way of defining who should receive a summons. In 1310, at least ninety were summoned; in 1375, the number was only forty-two; in 1378, twenty-eight; and in 1382 it had fallen to twenty. By then, however, the principle had been established that only those who held a barony were liable to be summoned, so that tenure of a barony became the hallmark of temporal peerage. It was this development which freed many magnates from the burden of attending parliament and which was responsible for the great reduction in the number of temporal peers sitting in the upper house (or house of lords, as it later became). The number had fallen so low by 1441 that the government became alarmed. By then peerage was a dignity which was highly esteemed and much sought, so that new peerages were only sparingly created. At the end of the middle ages there were only twelve peers in all, apart from the earls.

It is clear, then, that the numbers in each of the three 'houses' of parliament – the lords, the commons, and the lower clergy – were never very large. They tended, too, to be drawn mainly from the area which was most amen-

35

able to government control and influenced by the great
lords who in the later middle ages gained a grip on the
council. This dual character of parliament, its small size and
regional character, made it possible for the council to exercise a high measure of control over the assembly and its
procedure. He who controlled the council, therefore,
normally controlled the parliament – a fact which was used
to advantage by more than one chief governor in the latter
middle ages.

Taxation

Probably the most important business regularly transacted in parliament in the later middle ages was the granting
of necessary subsidies to the chief governor. In this the
commons naturally had an important part to play, since
it was the communities which they represented which
would carry the main burden of taxation. Right from the
beginning, therefore, when representatives of local communities were summoned to parliament to discuss taxation,
it was evident that their presence would not be advantage-
ous to the government if they did not have the power to
make a grant on behalf of their own constituencies. For
this reason a formula was worked out in the writs of
summons which required the communities to give to those
whom they elected to parliament full power (*plena potestas*)
to speak and act on their behalf. They were to be, in a very
literal sense, plenipotentiaries, so that whatever they con-
sented to in parliament would be subsequently binding on
their communities. Few more fundamental principles than
this one of representation were ever applied in medieval
Ireland. The local communities did not easily let go their
control over representatives, as the troubles of the era of
William of Windsor in the 1370s make plain. But by then
the principle behind parliamentary representation was well
established, together with the parliamentary subsidy.

The yield from these subsidies varied widely until they became standardised in the fifteenth century. In 1335, for example, a subsidy was granted which levied two shillings on each ploughland held by laymen, one shilling on each ploughland in clerical hands, a twentieth on the spiritualities of the clergy, and an unknown levy on movables (or chattels). In 1346 the grant was at the rate of two shillings a ploughland or on each £6 worth of movables, and a tenth on the spiritualities of the clergy. In 1371 there were two grants, £3,000 in January and £2,000 in June. This was highly exceptional, however, and produced an outcry which saw a radical change in the introduction of a custom, well established in the fifteenth century, of granting an annual subsidy of £700. By then, as we shall see, the area effectively governed from Dublin had shrunk to the Pale and the payment of substantial stipends (on paper at least) to the lieutenant further reduced the necessity for the making of lavish grants in parliament. In practice, however, the £700 was never fully collected and what was levied was slow to come in. No chief governor in the fifteenth century, therefore, could hope for much from the parliamentary subsidy, a fact which made his position all the more precarious financially.

There was some relief to be found, however, in the persistence of local taxation in Ireland, a custom which was really unknown in England. It was based on the well-established principle that normally the local community should be responsible for the cost of its own defence. In the fourteenth century the number of local subsidies increased and by the following century they were producing more than the annual parliamentary subsidy granted to the chief governor. Indeed, so important were they that parliament, increasingly conscious of its own authority, was attempting to gain control over local taxation in the early fifteenth century by enacting that parliamentary sanction was necessary for all local subsidies.

Revenues

The yield from most subsidies was trapped at source and expended locally, even where it was not rendered in kind. It did not, therefore, greatly augment exchequer revenues in the later middle ages. These were mainly derived from the traditional sources, the profits of justice, the royal demesne (including the towns), escheats and royal service (or scutage). Earlier, in the late thirteenth century, the yield from subsidies and the wool custom had considerably inflated revenues, so that for a time in the early 1290s exchequer income was more than £9,000 annually. But by the fourteenth century a drastic change had taken place, since revenue in the early years of the reign of Edward III had fallen to an annual average of only £1,200. It fluctuated afterwards, climbing to around £2,500 by the mid-century. Now that income from customs had more or less dried up, there was little hope of augmenting revenues further. They were sometimes artificially inflated by payments from England, but generally the annual income of the exchequer hovered around £2,000. During the fifteenth century, when the area effectively controlled by the government shrank to a small part of the island, annual revenues grew even smaller. During the two years ending at Michaelmas 1446, the treasurer, Giles Thorndon, accounted for less than £1,300. And in an official estimate of 1485, prepared after repeated requests by Richard III, an income of roughly £2,500 was arrived at by what were clearly over-generous allowances. Even so, practically all of that sum was trapped at source, so that less than £200 was left available to the chief governor.

The exchequer

All of this money was accounted for at the Dublin exchequer, even if little actual cash reached there in the late middle ages. The exchequer was the oldest department of state in Ireland and was certainly known by that name (in Latin, *scaccarium*) as early as 1200. But it must have existed even earlier, possibly from 1177 when John was made Lord of Ireland, under the official who later came to be known as the treasurer (first named as late as 1217). Throughout the thirteenth century the treasurer came next after the justiciar in the hierarchy of the Irish Government. He had a seat on the council and from quite early in the reign of Henry III he had a professional corps of officials and clerks staffing the two houses of the exchequer, the upper house, which was largely an accounting department and the lower house, which received and paid out money and receipts (or tallies). By the end of the thirteenth century the exchequer establishment had become fixed, the leading officials under the treasurer being the two chamberlains, the chancellor, barons (who audited the accounts and heard pleas at the exchequer court), two remembrancers (who were responsible for keeping the memoranda rolls, which together with the pipe rolls, chancellor's rolls, issue and receipt rolls, were the major regular records kept in the exchequer), an usher or doorkeeper, as well as engrossers (for writing the great rolls) and clerks.

As a result of a series of scandals, it was decided in the English parliament of 1293 that henceforth the Irish treasurer must have his accounts audited annually in England before the treasurer and the barons of the exchequer there. The audits, in fact, were not annual events and towards the end of the fourteenth century they tended to become more infrequent. By the Lancastrian period they were only occasionally held and they ceased altogether with the audit of Giles Thorndon's accounts in 1446. He was the last English trained official to be appointed to the office of treasurer and down to the time of the great financial reforms of the 1490s, the Irish exchequer (like the Irish administration in general) was independent of England.

But during that period when the treasurer was accountable in England, the Irish exchequer and Irish finances were under surveillance, however irregular, and some measure of control was exercised over the revenues at the disposal of the Irish government. Indeed the auditors in England were, if anything, too extreme in demanding full settlement of all outstanding sums. Tiny sums of only a shilling or, as in the extreme case of Robert of Embleton in 1350, of only three farthings, were relentlessly pursued until paid.

Another very important official, closely connected with the financial business of the king, was the escheator. His fee of £40 was equal to that of the treasurer, he had a seat in the council for many years, and the perquisites of office were very lucrative – in 1346, for example, Thomas of Exeter received 20s. from the sub-prior of Christ Church for executing a writ. Though he continued for a time to hold his place as next in importance after the chancellor and the treasurer (in 1346, for example, the justiciar was instructed to act in all important matters by the advice of the chancellor, treasurer and escheator), the decline in revenues from escheats gradually removed him from his important position in the official hierarchy. By the fifteenth century he had ceased to be a member of the council or an official of the first rank.

The chancery

Much more important, and taking precedence over the treasurer from 1291 onwards, was the chancellor. A separate Irish chancery was not established until 1232, when a royal great seal was provided for Ireland, under which writs were to be issued in the king's name. The organisation of the chancery followed, not only as an office for the writing of letters, but also for the keeping of copies which were enrolled on the patent and close rolls. Because the business of the chancery was more limited than that of the exchequer, its organisation was simpler and its staff more limited in number and quality. A keeper of the rolls is first recorded as late as the era of the Bruce invasion, and by the fifteenth century he had become a leading minister with a place in the council. Below him the number of clerks employed in the chancery remained small (on occasion as low as one and only in exceptional years reaching a maximum of six). Standards were generally low and there was difficulty in maintaining even the minimum staffing required. In 1364, for example, Henry of Leicester was released from prison in order to take up office in Ireland as keeper of the rolls. No wonder, then, that senior clerks had often to do the routine work which should have been seen to by juniors, in addition to the less ordinary work of writing out writs of summons to parliament, copying English statutes for circulation in Ireland, drafting reports on the state of Ireland or messages to the king from council or parliament.

As the official who had custody of the Irish great seal, which was used by the government to authenticate all important instruments of state, and without which the business of government could not be transacted, the chancellor naturally had to keep close to the chief governor, or his deputy, at all times. He therefore moved around the country with him, so that there was no fixed place in which the chancery was housed. Even during a military campaign, the chancellor would be found with the governor, often as leader of one of the retinues which made up the royal army. His cooperation was absolutely essential and on the infrequent occasions when he refused to make available the great seal to the chief governor, he could bring government to a halt. In July 1442, for example, the chancellor walked out of a council meeting, taking the seal with him. He sailed away to Wales and the seal disappeared for some time, until a friar, who said that it had been given to him in confession, brought it to the treasurer.

Local government

It was not enough for the chief governor to have a centralised administration through which he could govern. Regular contact had to be maintained with the local communities and this demanded a system of local government which would in effect extend the authority of the government into the localities. It was natural for the Anglo-Norman invaders to introduce into Ireland the system of local government with which they were familiar, based on the shire (divided in Ireland into cantreds and later into baronies) and the office of sheriff. Dublin was the first county, others following at intervals during the thirteenth century, so that by the early fourteenth century there were twelve in all: Dublin, Louth, Kildare, Meath, Carlow, Waterford, Roscommon, Connacht, Kerry, Cork, Limerick and Tipperary. Subsequently Carlow, Tipperary and Kerry became liberties, joining Ulster, Trim, Wexford and Kilkenny. But even within the liberties there were areas of church land (known as crosslands or crosses) which fell within the shire organisation of the lordship, each with its own sheriff in the later middle ages.

At first the sheriff was appointed by either the Irish or English government. But from the mid-fourteenth century he was elected by twenty-four 'of the best men' of the county. He was in the first place answerable to the exchequer for the collection of the royal revenue in his county, and was responsible for much local expenditure on behalf of the king and the Dublin Government. He presided over the county court, levied debts, brought people and pleas before the royal justices in eyre, looked after prisoners. It was as if he were an extension of the governor in the localities, transmitting royal commands, publishing statutes and ordinances, acting as police officer (with the help of the *posse comitatus*, 'the posse of the county'), and performing many necessary military functions in the county. He had, of course, many lesser officials to assist him and a body of clerks to keep records of all his transactions, especially those financial ones for which he was accountable at the Dublin exchequer.

In addition to sheriffs and their underlings, local government employed two major classes of official whose functions complemented the shire organisation: the coroner, whose main duty (as it still is) was to hold inquests on dead bodies, though he had many other duties to perform as well; and the keepers of the peace, who were concerned with both police duties and the making of war – it was they, for example, who made sure that those who were obliged to equip themselves with arms did so. They arrayed the shire levies and they commanded these forces in local warfare. Indeed, the functions of both these classes of official overlapped with those of the sheriff and they very often had to work together jointly.

It is important to remember, too, that within those areas which were organised as liberties, the lord (or his seneschal acting on his behalf) was expected to perform the functions of local government officials elsewhere. In this way the liberties were fitted into the system of local government, even though they had their own courts and their own internal organisations quite separate from those of the king.

The common law

The extension to Ireland of the common law system of England was of particular importance. It was the real basis of government. The foundations were really laid by King John, a crucial event being the council which met in his presence in Dublin, in 1210, at which the magnates of Ireland swore that the 'laws and customs' of England would be observed in Ireland. This was done 'by the common consent of all men of Ireland'. Royal courts and justices now applied the king's law side by side with the seignorial courts which were common to the whole feudal world. English statutes were sent to Ireland and applied in the courts. Of these courts, the most important was that of the justiciar, beyond which a plaintiff could appeal only to the king in England. The justiciar's court held sessions in different parts of the lordship, though less frequently in the later middle ages as the area in which the authority of the government was effective declined. There were itinerant justices, too, who went on eyre through the country, and from the middle of the thirteenth century there was a common bench (a court of 'common pleas') which remained permanently in Dublin, with a chief justice and its own records of pleas. By now the justices had become professionals, trained in the law, so that soon there was no place for the amateur (such as the chief governor normally was). There were, too, independent jurisdictions in the liberties, each with its own court, though even here certain pleas were reserved to the royal courts (rape, arson, forestalling, and treasure-trove), and in any case appeal could be made to the king in England.

One of the major flaws in this system was that it did not comprehend the whole of Ireland. The Gaelic Irish were excluded from the common law, being treated as aliens, except those who purchased charters of denizenship (and the so-called 'five bloods', the representatives of the five great ruling dynasties of pre-Norman Ireland). Those who lived in the Gaelic lordships were left under Brehon law; those in the colony were reduced to unfree status and were therefore denied the use of the royal courts. The Gaelic Irish were certainly discriminated against and suffered much inconvenience and many disabilities as a result. That their position worried them is evident from the attempt, in the late 1270s, of the Irish of Munster to purchase a grant of English law. Their failure, whether or not it was the result of opposition from the feudatories, was a disaster. In time attempts were made to extend English law to the whole of Ireland, most notably in 1331 after John Darcy had made this a precondition of his appointment as justiciar. An ordinance of that year stipulated that 'one and the same law be made as well for the Irish as the English'. But the legislation came too late to be effective. By then there was little interest among the Gaelic lordships, where the Brehon law system continued to flourish. With the expansion of Gaelic Ireland in the later middle ages, the Brehon Law area expanded too, pressing in upon the common law area.

The existence of what amounted to two separate areas of jurisdiction in the later middle ages naturally made government less effective. It was impossible, for example, to proceed adequately against felons who operated from bases in Gaelic Ireland (the 'land of war') where the king's writ did not run. When the government failed to give protection or to offer redress, its validity was in question. Individuals and communities had to be given licence to negotiate with felons, 'Irish enemies' and 'rebels of the king', to recover what they could as best they were able themselves. Sometimes they negotiated without licence, ignoring the rights of the government in the matter. People acted as go-betweens, passing from one jurisdiction to the other as mediators in the search for compensation. A famous instance was a woman of the O Tooles, called Grathagh le Deveneys in the record, who was 'accustomed at the request of the faithful men of peace, to go to the parts of the mountains, where she stays with women of the parts of peace, to see and search for cattle carried off by her race, that so men of peace may more easily recover their goods and cattle carried away'.

Compromises of this kind were bound to lead to an amalgam of two laws in some areas and to a toleration of actions taken 'in the manner of the marches', or what was known as march law (denounced by Edward I as 'detestable to God'). This was bound to further undermine the effectiveness of the government. Native custom inevitably influenced the common law and produced deviations from current practice in England. A famous example from 1299 shows the Rochefords proclaiming that the rule of primogeniture should not apply in default of male heirs, 'so that the inheritance shall never pass to daughters'. A parliament in 1310 applied the Brehon Law principle of kin responsibility to the Anglo-Irish magnates (significantly called 'chieftains of great lineage'). In 1316 it was complained that, again in accordance with Brehon law rules, fines were being taken for all felonies, even for the murder of Englishmen. The frequent condemnation of march law and Brehon law is a clear indication of how widespread was their use even in the land of peace.

Associated with this, though not derived from Gaelic custom, were the 'customs of the land of Ireland' which are frequently mentioned in contemporary records. These were old customs brought to Ireland by the early settlers, establishing local variations here of English customary law. Their validity was rarely questioned and they were tenaciously defended by the Anglo-Irish magnates, giving one basis for the growing separatist tendencies of the later middle ages.

The governance of medieval Ireland, then, was a replica of England's, with some local variations to suit the different circumstances in the lordship. But in practice, in the later middle ages, the system did not work very well, partly owing to the inadequacies of the officials, partly the result of a continuing tradition of peculation and malpractice in the administration, and also because there was a fairly rapid turnover in the personnel of a civil service which too often was regarded as a step towards higher office in England. But the real trouble was that this system was not suited to Ireland, which was never unified either politically or culturally. A centralised system of government was therefore ultimately unable to cope with the problems of a highly fragmented society.

3   A Land of War

Increasing lawlessness and disorder

In March 1375, the Mayor and citizens of Waterford, once one of the most prosperous and progressive settlements in Ireland, complained to the king 'of divers slaughters lately made by the king's enemies, to wit, of the mayor, bailiffs, sheriff, coroner, clerk and twenty-six of the better men of the city as well as eighty men of England, from Coventry, Dartmouth, Bristol and other ports of England, and six weeks afterwards of twenty-four of the better men of the city'. The city was in a perilous condition. 'The country round is despoiled, burned and destroyed up to the walls'. Communication with the outside world was becoming increasingly difficult, even by sea. The expansion of the land of war, and the failure of the government to cope with the problem, was cutting off towns like Waterford. There were large tracts of land where the law was scarcely enforced and where the king's writ was hardly effective. Lawlessness increased and local disorder became common. For this the local communities blamed the inadequacies of the government and the failure of chief governors to discharge their duties locally. Another Waterford petition, this time from 1441, described how the Powers were causing havoc in the city and its hinterland: 'from day to day [they] ride in the manner of war with banners displayed and rob, spoil and kill the king's liegemen'. The real cause of this, it was said, was 'that the lieutenant and governors of this land for the time being have not continually used to reside in the parts of Waterford and in default of chastisement of the said traitors and rebels, according to the law of the king, the said city is for the greater part destroyed and laid waste'.

This complaint echoed what had been said to Pope John XXII in 1331 in an official communiqué from the Irish council which confessed that the king's justice could not be administered by the royal officials because they went in fear of death. Admittedly, this was an attempt to invoke papal aid in a crusade against the enemies of the king in Ireland and we might therefore expect it to paint a lurid picture of the poor state of Ireland and of the Irish Church. But what a terrible admission it contains that the rule of law was breaking down, with government officials unable (or unwilling) to discharge their duty. There is plenty of evidence that this was the case. Parliamentary legislation (such as that of 1297, or 1310, or 1320) illustrates well how bad things were at the beginning of the century. Much of it is concerned with absenteeism, civil war, degeneracy, local defence, and the increasing lawlessness in the localities. Lawlessness and disorder were in evidence all over the lordship. It was no longer safe to move around the country. Even royal officials had to receive adequate protection. In August 1349, when the chancellor went to Connacht, taking the great seal with him, he was allowed to have eight men at arms and seven archers over and above the retinue which he normally retained, 'for the safety of the said seal'. The Kilkenny parliament of 1310 was told by a special commission established to inquire into a sudden rise in prices that 'merchants, strangers and others passing through the country are robbed of their goods by those of great lineage, against whom they had frequently heretofore had small means of recovery'.

Reliance on the magnates

In its attempt to cope with the problems, the government

tended to rely heavily on the magnates, reminding them of their responsibilities, as happened in 1355, when a letter sent out on 5 June ordered the earl of Kildare to defend the march of Kildare. There was nothing new in this in principle. In the thirteenth century the magnates had been heavily involved in peace-keeping operations. Occasionally royal service had been granted to them to help keep out Irish enemies who were pressing on certain marches. Just how important the local magnate was is vividly illustrated by a message sent to the king by a great council which met at Kilkenny in 1360. Complaining of the effects of the Black Death ('so great and hideous among the English lieges') and of the failure of absentees to maintain their lands, it emphasised the lack of great lords who used to defend the marches in the absence of the justiciar. The problem was aggravated by the disappearance of so many of the leading families before the end of the first quarter of the fourteenth century. Earlier the Lacy families in Meath and Ulster, and the Marshal family in Leinster, had died out in the male line. Their heirs subsequently died out: de Clare, lord of Kilkenny; de Vescy, lord of Kildare; de Valence, lord of Wexford; de Verdon, lord of part of Meath; and Bigod, lord of Carlow. The removal of so many great names may have made it easier for others, such as the Geraldines and Butlers, to come to the fore. But it had a disastrous effect on the feudal settlement in many areas.

Relying on the local lords meant that the government had to tolerate a degree of independence which in other circumstances would have been intolerable. During the Bruce invasion a number of people had been given general pardons on condition that they did not assist the Scots, a sad indication of the government's inability to take stern measures against the breakers of the peace. In 1319 four commissioners, including the famous John Wogan who had long served both Edward I and Edward II as justiciar in Ireland, were appointed to make inquiry into Bruce's Irish supporters. But the following year they gave up the investigation. We are not told why, but obviously they were discovering too much for comfort.

The local magnate had to be allowed to proceed in his own way, provided some measure of peace was preserved in his locality. The old principle that there should be 'one war and one peace' in the lordship (that is, that only the government should declare war or make peace and that all local communities must abide by this) was still maintained; but it was slowly giving way to the realities of life in fourteenth-century Ireland. More and more the local lord and the local community had to be empowered to work out a *modus vivendi* with the local Gaelic community. Only by thus delegating its rights in peace and war could the central government retain some measure of control over relations between the two peoples in late medieval Ireland. Thus, in the period after the Bruce invasions, there is a notable increase in the number of licences to 'parley' with Irish enemies. For example, on 13 July 1319 Hugh Lawless 'and other faithful of his kin' had a patent to 'treat and parley with Irish of the name of Mac Murrough and O Toole and O Byrne of Leinster'. Such treaties could still be regulated. A 1337 treaty of peace between the community of Louth and Donal O Hanlon was formally drawn up in the form of a public instrument by a public notary, so that terms would be observed. Thus, when the peace was broken the government commissioned four men to cause inquiry to be made as to how the terms agreed to were broken.

The clan system

One of the most extraordinary examples of the government relying on the magnates for upholding the rule of law was the extension of the Irish legal principle of kin responsibility to them. This law of *cin comhfhocuis* was applied by statute in 1278 to the Gaelic communities in the common law area. Then in 1310 'every chieftain of great lineage' (the heads of the great Anglo-Irish families) was made responsible for those of his name who broke the peace; and in 1324 the great lords agreed to arrest law-breakers 'of their own family and surname'. The earls of Kildare, Ulster, and Louth, together with fourteen other lords, solemnly put their seals to this undertaking in writing, thus extending a Brehon law principle at the highest level of society and explicitly recognising the existence of a clan system among the settlers no less than among their Gaelic neighbours. Contemporary records refer constantly to the 'nations' (*naciones*) of Anglo-Ireland, or to the great families (*cognomina*), as if indeed they were clans. The Kilkenny chronicler Friar Clyn, writing in the first half of the four-teenth century, talks of the *naciones et cognomina* ('nations and families') of the Geraldines and Powers. The Irish council in 1399 reported on *les nacions Engleis* ('the English nations') such as the Butlers, Powers, Geraldines, Ber-minghams, Daltons, Baretts and Dillons, who were not amenable to law. Indeed, occasionally the government actually gave official recognition to heads of family chosen by election, as was the case with the Harolds of south Dublin, by formally accepting each one as *capitaneus nacionis sue* ('captain of his nation'), in exactly the same way as they formally recognised elected Gaelic chieftains. An official record of 1377, for example, tells us that Turloch O Brien had been 'made captain of his nation by the council of Ireland'. In 1350, John Byrne, 'captain elect of his nation' took oath of office before the justiciar and promised that should any of his name commit a crime he would bring them to account. The hope was, presumably, that such official recognition would perhaps strengthen the chieftain and stabilise his position, making him a useful agent for peace.

In the same way the great lords, too, worked through the clan system in order to build up alliances and preserve some sort of order in the localities. The earl of Ormond, in 1359, made a contract with O Brennan, whereby the latter swore to serve him against Irish enemies and English rebels and to keep the peace. Sometimes, of course, agreements of this kind did not work to the advantage of the government. As the fourteenth century progressed, references to confederations of Irish and English became more frequent.

Rebel English and factions

Usually, however, those who confederated with Irish enemies were rebel English, whose numbers grew in the fourteenth century until they became as great, or even a greater, nuisance than the Irish themselves – a fact which was commented on in a 1346 report to the king on the state of Ireland, which stated: 'there are serious disturbances in various parts of Ireland and between the English, which are more harmful to the king's fortunes than the wars with the Irish'. In May 1320, for example, an army had to be sent to Munster against 'rebels John fitz Thomas fitz Maurice and David de Barry and their followers, namely of the name of Burke and Barry'. The Burkes, of course, are the classic case. Refusing to accept the operation of the common law after the murder of the last earl of Ulster in 1333, so that his vast inheritance passed to his daughter and through her to an absentee, the junior de Burghs occupied most of Mayo and Galway, changed their name to the Irish form 'Burke', and held on to their lordships there. When Lionel of Clarence died in 1368, in law the rightful lord of these usurped lands, an inquisition recorded the melancholy fact that all those manors which used to be worth £200 a year to the duke were now worth nothing, 'because they are occupied by Edmund de Burgo knight and other rebels of the king, both English and Irish, nor has any minister of the king dared to go thither to execute his office'. The Lacys and de Verdons in Meath are other examples of rebels who were dissatisfied with the feudal law of primogeniture. The de Berminghams, who took the name Mac Pheorais ('son of Piers'), are yet another example.

It is easy to sympathise with the view that the operation of primogeniture often led to inheritance by heiresses, the fragmentation (and therefore the weakening) of lordships, and absentee lords. Some families were determined that this would not happen and took the necessary precautions. A most remarkable example, as we have already seen, is the proclamation issued in 1299 by the Rocheford family that the barony of Ikeathy in county Kildare would not be partitioned in default of a male heir in the male line, but would go to the strongest Rocheford, 'so that the inheritance shall never pass to daughters'.

For the most part, however, the junior branches of families who became rebel English did so for the simplest of motives: greed for land. If they could not inherit legally, then they would occupy illegally. A 'memorial' from the city and county of Cork in the mid-fourteenth century described the ruin that threatened Munster because of the dissensions among the Carews, Barnewalls, de Courcys, Arundels and other families who had fallen 'at variance among themselves; the weakest took Irishmen to their aid and so vanquished the enemies'. Not only did they ally with Irish enemies to achieve their ends, they often formed confederations among themselves and terrorised the countryside. Complaints against such gangs were frequent and parliamentary legislation and royal ordinances did little to stop them. Frequently, too, the disaffected attached themselves to the households of the greater lords, helping to build up the factions which were to be such an agent for lawlessness in the localities.

As with the rebel English, these factions sometimes allied with Gaelic chieftains who were pressing in on the land of peace. In 1329, for example, the de Lacys joined with the Mac Geoghans and killed Sir Thomas Butler and others near Mullingar. Faction fights could easily shade into civil

53

war, involving great magnates, or they might mirror factional interest in England. The supporters of Mortimer and Despenser, for example, fought it out in Ireland. The liberty of Kilkenny was held by Hugh Despenser and he had as his seneschal there Arnold le Poer (long since a figure of some notoriety – in 1307 a Kildare parliament had to make peace between him and the relatives of John de Boneville, whom he had slain). Roger Mortimer was lord of Trim and other Irish estates besides. Le Poer was supported most prominently by the de Burghs; the opposition, backing Mortimer, consisted of the Geraldines (always in opposition to the de Burghs), the Butlers, and the Berminghams. In 1326 an attempt to reconcile the parties failed. The following year both Maurice fitz Thomas on the one side and Arnold le Poer on the other were ordered to stop raising men at arms and foot-soldiers to attack each other. In 1326 no less than four sheriffs were ordered to forbid 'rebellions, conventions and conspiracies'. But it was all to no avail and by 1327 the factions were openly at war. Contemporary opinion, reflected in Anglo-Irish chronicles, was that Maurice fitz Thomas had been insulted by le Poer, who used 'monstrous language' about him: he called him a *rymour*, the kind of insult no decent Anglo-Irishman could tolerate. But the real cause went deeper and the conflict did not end (despite the efforts of a Kilkenny parliament in 1327, or an order of the English council in June 1328 that the feud between the Geraldines was to be suppressed) until Arnold le Poer died (in 1329) and Roger Mortimer was executed (in 1330). In 1329 the earl of Louth, John de Bermingham, was murdered at Braganstown in county Louth, together with a large number of kinsmen and followers. Contemporary opinion was that this had no connexion with the fitz Thomas/ le Poer war, in which the de Berminghams had been heavily involved, but was purely a local matter. Another famous murder, that of the earl of Ulster in 1333, was also an expression of local dissensions and it is also a good example of the great harm which local faction fights could cause to the community. For the murder had disastrous consequences for the great lordships of Ulster and Connacht.

One bizarre manifestation of the great Mortimer/Despenser quarrel in Ireland was the trial for witchcraft of Alice Kyteler and others in Kilkenny. The bishop of Ossory, who for reasons known only to himself had become involved with the pro-Mortimer faction, charged Alice in 1324 with sorcery and before long many of the most important and wealthiest people in Kilkenny were involved, including the seneschal Arnold le Poer. Even the deputy justiciar, head of the government, was charged with heresy. The bishop undoubtedly was eccentric – for example, he carried the sacred Host on himself regularly, so that an attack on his person would be an attack on the Body of Christ – and there may have been strange motives behind these charges, which resulted in the execution at the stake of at least one person. But there seems little doubt that the attack on le Poer was connected with the great contemporary faction fight.

The most notorious example of faction war is provided by Maurice fitz Thomas (created first earl of Desmond in 1329) and his 'rout', which terrorised large areas for years. He employed the old Gaelic custom of *cáin* (anglicised *coyne*) which allowed him to claim sustenance (either food or money) for his troops from his people. In this way he built up a formidable body of retainers. His early success made others flock to join him ('English as well as Irish . . . from Connacht and Thomond, from Leinster and Desmond' according to later indictments) and they, too, were encouraged to despoil the countryside of food and drink, often far outside Desmond's own lordship. Important Anglo-Irishmen, like Sir Robert fitz Matthew de Caunton, Sir Maurice fitz Philip and Sir Thomas fitz Gilbert joined him. So did some great Gaelic lords, like Brian O Brien,

Dermot Mac Carthy, William Carrach O Brien. They raided, harried, destroyed and seized booty wherever they could all over the south. They went to war against the Roches, Barrys and Cogans. Finally the earl made it known that he had higher ambitions: a jury at Limerick declared that 'Maurice's heart had been greatly exalted for fully five years, and his ambition and acquisitiveness were such that he had planned to obtain the whole of Ireland for himself and to have himself crowned king'. On 7 July 1326 there was an extraordinary meeting in county Tipperary, attended by the earl of Kildare, the earl of Louth, James Butler (future earl of Ormond), fitz Thomas (shortly to be earl of Desmond) and the bishop of Ossory among others, at which a great rebellion against the king and a takeover of Ireland was planned. It was agreed that fitz Thomas should be crowned king and the others would share Ireland in proportion to the military contribution they made to the rebellion. This preposterous scheme came to nothing, but it showed the way Desmond's ambition grew. It was probably also an outcome of the Mortimer/Despenser war, with Desmond making the most of his chances.

It is impossible to condense the full story of Desmond's rebellious career – the destruction he caused, the loss of life, the repeated defiance of all royal officials (including a later plot, using Gaelic lords such as O Brien and Macnamara, in addition to Anglo-Irish magnates, to make Desmond king of Ireland), his involvement with Irish enemies and other English rebels, his attempt to persuade the kings of France and Scotland to make war on the English and to help him to conquer Ireland, his offer to pay 3,000 marks annually to the pope for Ireland. He was finally forced into submission in 1346, stood trial in England, and was freed on a legal technicality. He had already been pardoned for his treason and his estates and title were restored. Finally, a fantastic end to a career of treason, rebellion and crime, he was appointed justiciar of Ireland in the summer of 1355.

Problems of degeneracy

Desmond was also typical of that degeneracy which was feared by the government and regularly condemned. Many of the early settlers had married Irish women, so that their children were half Gaelic, speaking the language and naturally acquiring from their mothers an orientation towards Gaelic culture. The habit of intermarriage persisted at every level of society, through successive generations, making it difficult (and in the end impossible) for many families to retain their English cultural inheritance intact. As Irish customs, habits and speech spread, especially after the Gaelic revival made possible a reconquest of lost territories and a resumption of lost lordships, the alarm of the government expressed itself in a whole series of parliamentary enactments from 1297 – when the term degenerate (*degeneres*) was first used of those English who had adopted certain Irish habits – climaxed by the famous statutes of Kilkenny of 1366. An ordinance issued in the king's name by the justiciar, the earl of Ormond, on 3 February 1360, under the great seal of Ireland makes clear what the government feared most. It complains that 'many men of the English nation both in the marches of our land of Ireland and elsewhere there have recently assumed the condition of Irishmen', renouncing English laws and customs and embracing Irish, taking preys and holding 'parleys in the Irish fashion', speaking Irish and fostering their children with Irishmen ('so that they may drink in, love and use the Irish language'), degenerating and for the most part becoming Irish 'to the manifest diminution of our lordship of the said land'. All of this is now forbidden, 'on pain of losing English liberty' and must cease by 24 June following.

Even as early as the reign of King John, Giraldus Cambrensis had reported the 'folly' and the 'arrogance and presumption' of some of the new settlers who 'aspire to usurp in their own persons all the rights of dominion belonging to the princes of that kingdom'. We have seen how the first earl of Desmond assumed such rights. There was obviously danger in degeneracy. But there was no way of stopping it. The greatest in the land succumbed to the language, literature and the arts of Gaelic Ireland. They kept court poets, as did the Gaelic lords, and accepted the flattery of praise-poems and occasionally the urgings to seek glory. A fifteenth-century poem addressed to Walter Burke of Connacht urged him to conquer new lands: 'Folk blame you for tarrying on the confines of Connacht; marchlands befit you not; let us stretch forward to the centre of Eire'. They often accepted the Brehon law, or what was known as march law, at the expense of the common law, which naturally made the task of administrators nearly impossible. For, as a fourteenth-century ordinance trenchantly put it, 'where there is a diversity of law the people cannot be of one law or one community'. From degeneracy it was but a short step to rebellion and this was one reason why successive governments tried to control the problem. But there was no real answer short of resettlement, or plantations of the kind attempted in the early modern period, so that the English language and way of life might be invigorated. And no medieval government was able, or prepared, to take such a drastic step.

Absentees

Another problem which preoccupied the government was that of absenteeism. The message from the Kilkenny great council of 1360 to the king complained bitterly of the failure of absentees to maintain and guard their lands. This was a long-standing problem. The parliament of 1297, which devoted much time to the problem of defence in the marches had focussed attention on the dangerous neglect of lands in the marches, 'whereby very many marches are either altogether destroyed or are for the greater part ruinous, and the English inhabitants either obey felons or are

driven as it were into exile'. It also condemns those 'magnates and others who reside in England or elsewhere out of
this land, who cause the profits of their land to be trans-
mitted to them from this land, leaving nothing here to
protect their tenements or the tenants thereof'. From then
on there were frequent complaints of the effects of absenteeism. Those who remained in Ireland always maintained
that lands 'were wasted and occupied by the king's enemies
there for want of custody', as Edward III expressed it in a
letter of 15 October 1331 to the earl of Norfolk, one of the
great absentees. In ordering Norfolk to provide 'for the
safe custody' of his lands in Ireland, the king warned him
that he himself was going on expedition to Ireland and if he
'find the earl's lands in the hands of the enemy and cause
them to be delivered by armed force, he may have his will
of the said lands as being of his own conquest'. This principle of confiscation had already been applied. In the
summer of 1327, for example, the Irish government was
ordered to use the profits of the lands of absentees to provide an adequate guard (to keep them 'in strength').

Edward III denounced those who 'have caused the issues
and profits of their lands to be carefully collected, making
no provision for their defence'. These were the ones who
could be got at. An ordinance of 1351 showed what could be
done: if anyone failed to provide an adequate defence for
lands in the marches, then 'the issues of their lands in the
land of peace shall be taken by the king's ministers and
expended in the march for the safeguard of the said march'.
Quite regularly chief governors ordered individuals to
return to the marches and provide adequate protection for
their lands, so that neighbours should not suffer. When
Maurice fitz Thomas, earl of Kildare, was ordered to join
in the guarding of his own marches, the letter to him
emphasised his obligation and threatened 'forfeiture of
your body and all your lands in the said county granted by
the Crown'. When Thomas de Rokeby went on campaign

and recovered land from Gaelic lords such as Mac Dermot, he 'proclaimed that all Englishmen should return to the devastated lands within forty days and reside, or forfeit'. In the same way, when Lionel of Clarence was campaigning in the 1360s he, too, ordered absentees to return to lands which he had 'by great war acquired'.

There is plenty of evidence that firm action was taken by the Irish government in cases such as these. For example, the lands of John Crophull near Dundalk were confiscated and then let to farm, because he did not defend them in person or with sufficient men. At one stage, during the period when William of Windsor was in office, an attempt was made to impose royal service on lands which had been occupied by the Irish. But however vigorous any government was in its attempts to impose sanctions, or to find a solution to the problem of absentees, it never succeeded in deriving a sufficient income to protect adequately the neglected march lands, or in forcing absentees resident in England to accept responsibility for neglected estates in Ireland. Early in the reign of Richard II this was tacitly recognised in an English statute when the penalty prescribed was a levy of two-thirds of the profits or rents of the land, benefice or other source of profit which had been neglected. This was aimed at those who derived an assessable income from Ireland and was primarily directed against beneficed clergy. That this was realised is demonstrated by the swift clerical reaction, when the bishops attempted to argue that the clergy could not be bound by a statute to which they had not given their consent and which came from a parliament to which they had not been summoned. Apart from the interesting constitutional point this raised, it showed a full realisation of the effect of this statute on the clergy, so many of whom had to absent themselves from Ireland to study at the theological schools, to do business at the papal court, to go on pilgrimage, or for many other good reasons. But despite the protest, the law was vigorously imposed, was confirmed by Henry IV shortly after his accession, and remained in force to the end of the middle ages.

The Gaelic revival

The attempt to overcome the dangers caused by absenteeism by means of legislation failed. The Gaelic lords continued to press in on abandoned or inadequately defended lands and the common law area continued to shrink. A great Gaelic recovery of lost lordships was taking place and this is reflected in much of the record evidence from the fourteenth century. It had begun long since. The advance of the feudal area in the thirteenth century is attested in a most striking fashion in the annals, where a new style of writing, borrowed from the Anglo-Normans, is employed. But later there is a return of Irish forms, indicating a Gaelic cultural revival. For the Gaelic recovery was not just one of military conquest, but of arts and letters too. The poets were conscious of this and expressed it in their poetry. They were also conscious that a Gaelic Ireland was being restored: 'Ireland is a woman who has risen again from the horrors of reproach' and she now belongs to Irishmen again. Others encouraged their patrons to win glory, urging them to rely on their own strength, and not to depend any longer on charters or the like: 'Seek no other charter except thy own reliance on thy gallantry'. A fourteenth-century poem to an O Connor exhorts him to make a bid for the high kingship: ' . . . our hope is fixed on another fair on bright-surfaced Teamhair'. This, of course, was nonsense, since the failure of Edward Bruce ended the high kingship for all time. But it is not difficult to see that flattering poetry of this kind must have inspired many a Gaelic lord to strike out for glory.

The disturbed conditions produced by the Bruce wars had given many Gaelic lords their chance and they seized it with gusto. In the battle of Dysert O Dea in 1318 Richard de Clare was defeated and killed by the O Briens and the independence of a Gaelic Thomond was virtually assured. The O Connors in Connacht and O Neills in the north exploited the situation in their own interest. In the south, the Mac Carthys had long since consolidated their position in Desmond. The Mac Murrough kingship was revived in Leinster and during the later middle ages the dynasty succeeded in consolidating its position in the south of the province, while exercising some degree of overlordship over Gaelic lords to the north and west of them. Of these, the O Tooles of the Wicklow mountains and the O Byrnes further north were particularly aggressive and independent. The O Connors of Offaly and the O Mores of Leix held great lordships in the midlands, maintaining continuous pressure on the land of peace. Indeed, when they acted in conjunction with Mac Murrough or Gaelic lords from the mountains, they were a serious menace to the settlements in the Pale. In Connacht it was the degenerate Burkes (the two Mac William families) who were by far the most powerful. Mac Dermot, together with the Sligo branch of the O Connors, was the greatest Gaelic lord. There were, of course, many lesser lords who played a prominent part in the tangled politics of the later middle ages – O Kelly and O Madden in the west, O Reilly and O Rourke in Brefny, O Farrell in Longford, O Carroll in Ely, O Melaghlin of Westmeath, Maguire of Fermanagh, Mac Mahon of Oriel and, most important of all, O Donnell of Tirconnell. Until the later fifteenth century the latter family was only rarely and marginally involved in the politics of Anglo-Ireland.

Fall in revenues

The expansion of Gaelic Ireland at the expense of the land of peace naturally meant a decline in the revenues paid into the Dublin exchequer. If courts cannot function, the

profits of justice must disappear. Where local administration breaks down, revenues cease to be forwarded to the
exchequer. A sheriff was appointed in Connacht in the
later middle ages, but he never accounted at the exchequer.
The escheator never collected profits from escheats there.
No tax could be assessed or collected. Feudal incidents disappeared. During the fourteenth century, when there
seems to have been a trade recession as a result of the disturbed conditions in the lordship and the high population
losses, income from customs practically disappeared. The
wool custom, which in the thirteenth century had been one
of the most lucrative sources of revenue to the government,
virtually produced nothing. A special custom on all exports
(especially fish, wine, beef and pork) granted to William of
Windsor in 1369 was effective in only a small number of
ports in the east and produced only minor sums: the
account of the collector, Roger de Leases, in the city of
Dublin, Drogheda, and counties Louth, Meath, Kildare
and Waterford for the period 8 August 1369 to 21 January
1370 covered only four ports – Dublin ($£40.9.7\frac{1}{2}$);
Drogheda ($£11.7.0\frac{3}{4}$); Carlingford ($£8.0.0$); Waterford
($£16.3.9$).

It is important to stress that the fall in government
income in the early part of the fourteenth century had been
not far short of catastrophic. During the reign of Edward I
the income recorded in the final, audited accounts of the
Irish treasurers, show a receipt which was somewhat in excess of $£6,000$ (though it fell at times to just over $£5,000$).
These figures do not reveal the real income of the government, since they do not fully record local expenditure
which may not appear in the audited account. But they are
a safe index to revenues for purposes of comparison. In the
reign of Edward II a startling decline is evident: from
$£3,500$ to $£2,300$. For most of the fourteenth century it
hovered around the $£2,000$ level. In other words, income
fell to about one-third of what it had been during the most

prosperous era of the lordship. No government could afford such a loss and still maintain a rule of law.

In fourteenth-century Ireland, it meant that the problem of defence, made particularly acute by the Gaelic revival and the increased activity of the rebel English, became too much for the government. Lack of money resulted in a failure to maintain castles or garrisons in frontier areas. It often meant that it was impossible to pay soldiers or provide victuals. In August 1368 the chancellor was awarded a special grant of £43.6.8, for his labour and expenses in finding men at arms and other troops 'to resist the O Tooles at a time when the treasury was empty of money'. In September 1374, the bishop of Meath was to go to Munster with an army to help Mac Namara. 'And because the king has nothing in his treasury of Ireland, nor would he have in the future, to maintain war', it was ordained and agreed by the council that the bishop was to try and persuade the local communities to grant a subsidy. If a subsidy were not granted, then the bishop was to seize 'corn and animals, for his victuals and expenses', in each county of Munster, to be paid for later by the sheriffs. In April 1335, John Cadde, with a small force of men, was also sent to Munster to defend certain areas; again, lack of money made it necessary for the council to empower him to seize 'all kinds of victuals for his sustenance'. Examples could be multiplied.

It was for this reason that gradually in the fourteenth century the Irish government became financially dependent on England. At a critical stage during the Bruce invasion, a special envoy of the king in Ireland, John of Hotham, sent an urgent appeal for money. From then on the Irish government had to be subsidised, increasingly with the passing years. In two letters Edward III expresses his attitude forcefully: in one he complained that he had 'incurred great cost and expenses upon the upkeep of the war in Ireland without taking any revenues or profits therefrom, and neither the king nor his subjects of England can comfortably bear these expenses in the same way as they bore those formerly occasioned by the wars with France and Spain'; in a second letter he said that he 'cannot support such expenses any more, especially as he has divers wars elsewhere'. The king did make a massive investment in Ireland during the 1360s and 1370s, when first Clarence and then William of Windsor tried to prop up the tottering lordship. Subsequently chief governors were also heavily subsidised – most notably Gloucester, appointed in 1392, who was to receive 34,000 marks for three years; and Surrey, appointed in 1398, who was promised 11,000 marks a year.

Peculation and corruption

The Irish government, then, could only maintain a defence of the frontier with the financial support of the English taxpayer. Even in day to day administration, however, insufficiency of money led to a default in the payment of salaries and fees. This had the effect of increasing official peculation, since many royal officials (especially in the localities) made sure of recouping themselves at the expense of the local community and the king's exchequer. Naturally, this did not make for efficient administration. The difficulties of the government were added to by the defection of many royal officials to England without accounting and owing money. In 1348, for example, nine former ministers (including three escheators and two sheriffs) were found to have defaulted. Some owed very large sums: John Dufford, a former excheator, owed £712; David Caunton, a former sheriff of Cork, owed £219. But the difficulties of tracing most errant officials in England made it impossible to recover the debts. Even in the thirteenth century this had presented a problem. In 1281 the justiciar, Stephen of Fulbourn, named sheriffs who, he claimed, had extorted money from individuals in their counties and then left Ireland. They lose nothing, he said, because they 'have nothing to be distrained by' and so they cannot be made to pay for their crimes.

This tradition of local peculation persisted and, up to a point, was tolerated. It was expected that royal officials would augment their incomes by private dealings. The fact that local office was much sought after, particularly that of sheriff, in spite of the legitimate rewards of office not being great, means that the holders of offices found much scope for peculation and picked up many a shilling through bribes and what we today would call 'protection money'. For example, William Austyn and John Clement, king's serjeants in county Limerick in 1295, 'summoned poor tenants for the county court . . . and to inquisitions, and for reward allowed the rich to remain at home; and they summoned and attacked poor persons of the county to come to the county court . . . without precept, and afterwards took reward from them to let them go home. And they levied fines from those from whom they ought not to levy. And they prosecuted summons upon free tenants who were not summoned. And when commanded to attach felons, they let them go for bribes'. Sheriffs regularly took bribes from people to exempt them from jury service. Some retained for themselves chattels which they were empowered to seize for debts. A serjeant in Kilmallock, county Limerick, 'took a mare of Walter son of Adam as distraint for a debt of the king and brought it to his own house and detained it for four days in his own work, and on the fifth day it died, to the damage of Walter of 4s'. Sheriffs revealed names of juries to those indicted, in return for a suitable reward. Others extorted money by force from local communities, suppressed writs which endangered their own interests, suppressed indictments for cash payments, and had people who refused to bribe them, and especially their enemies, indicted and imprisoned without cause. In fact the use of what was called 'duress of prison' was a very popular way of extracting money from innocent people. And of course sheriffs used the same weapon with criminals – one in county Limerick released a prisoner from his jail in return for a large number of cows which the criminal gave him. Yet another way of procuring money was by taking bribes from people threatened with appointment to the unpopular and profitless office of coroner.

The prevailing wartime conditions, and in particular the operation of purveyance, gave an opportunity which few officials missed. In 1311, for example, a purveyor was found guilty of seizing 'on his own authority and without warrants' the wheat of certain people. Then, in exchange for different sums of money ($\frac{1}{2}$ mark from one, 40d. from another, and so on) he returned the wheat to the owners. The justiciar's court at Ardfert, county Kerry, on 12 June 1307, was told how a local sub-serjeant and others were ordered to purvey cattle locally. This they did, but returned some to owners who were willing to pay sums (called 'extortion' in the court record) varying from 3d. to 6d. Examples such as this could be multiplied.

There were many scandals, too, among the higher civil servants, particularly in the exchequer (where standards of probity should have been especially high). One treasurer after another was charged with falsifying accounts, making payments without warrant, issuing false acquittances, not issuing tallies, often in collusion with lesser officials who were supposed to be keeping check on them. Even the royal justices were corrupt. A fierce indictment of the chief ministers came from the king in 1336 in a letter to the chancellor and treasurer. In it he said that 'it has been shown to the king by honest men of those parts and public fame proclaims that the justiciar, chancellor and treasurer and the other ministers and officers of the king there are respectors of persons and do not treat the powerful, middle and simple men of that land by an equal law, but show too great favour to the powerful, permitting them to oppress the poor, to invade the king's rights, to usurp the royal power, to detain the king's debts, to institute novelties and perpetrate various crimes'.

The problem of defence

Corruption, inefficiency, lack of money all made the business of government difficult in the extreme. The Gaelic revival, the increase in the numbers of rebel English, the growth of absenteeism and the high incidence of lawlessness and disorder meant that too much time had to be devoted to the problem of defence and of peace-keeping in the localities. If the lordship were to survive in any real sense, then a system of defence had to be worked out which would come within the capacity of fourteenth-century governments. Making war placed a terrible strain on local communities, not least because they suffered (as non-combatants always do) from the passage of armies. In 1311, for example, when an army was sent to protect Louth, the local community asserted 'that by the coming of so great an army, the faithful men of these parts would suffer greater evils than before' and asked to be allowed to guard the county themselves. Such offers were extremely rare, however, and while employing the age-old system of local defence which had been brought to Ireland by the earliest invaders, the government on the whole had to assume responsibility for the making of war at all levels.

It is important to realise that, with very few exceptions, no official war in medieval Ireland was fought with conquest in mind. Very often they were defensive wars. And where the government took the offensive, its purpose usually was not to engage the enemy in battle and defeat him, but rather to force him into submission by exercising pressure upon his lands and people. The methods employed might vary from time to time and place to place; but most commonly the destruction of crops, buildings and chattels, mainly through fire, was of far more importance than the slaughter of troops. People lived so nearly at subsistence level that it was easy enough to plunge them below it. The taking of preys of cattle became almost as much a part of Anglo-Ireland as it traditionally was of Gaelic Ireland. Indeed, and almost inevitably, Gaelic custom exercised a considerable influence on the waging of war. The taking of hostages, for example, became a normal feature of war, as did the employment of mercenaries (usually Gaelic) by the government.

The typical pattern of warfare was to employ small forces, with very limited objectives. This helped to keep costs down. But even small forces could be too expensive for an impoverished government, if kept in the field for any length of time. Between 20 April and 27 July 1349 Walter de Bermingham was employed with a small retinue of 10 men at arms and 50 archers, but the wages bill came to over £122. Amory de St Armand while chief governor, had 40 men at arms (of whom only 10 were knights) and 100 mounted archers beyond the 20 men at arms which every justiciar was obliged to maintain. The extra wages for one year, 27 February 1358 to 26 February 1359, came to more than £1,516. No Irish government could afford this for very long.

A system of warding, or guarding fixed points with small forces, was extensively employed by the government, especially in Leinster. Sometimes the obligation of maintaining the ward was placed on the local community or the local magnates. But frequently the cost fell on the exchequer and if the period of warding was extensive (as it often was) the expense was high. A very famous example, unusually well documented, comes from the late thirteenth century when the head of the government, John of Sandford, set up a series of wards around the marches of Leix and Offaly. He, himself, with 17 men at arms (all squires) and 60 footmen took responsibility for two wards. Small as his force was, it cost more than £580 during the year the wards lasted. What might therefore have been an ideal way of keeping watch on trouble spots, so that any Gaelic rising could be anticipated and perhaps even prevented, proved to be too expensive to be widely employed or permanently maintained. Too often, for want of money, wards had to be disbanded.

The English government and Ireland

For major military enterprises, then, the Irish government looked to England for help. It was important, therefore, that regular communication should be maintained and that the king and his council should be informed on Irish affairs. Messengers to and from England were frequent. Reports were sent from Ireland by the king's ministers on the state of the lordship. Petitions of grievance, appeals for help, condemnations of ministers were forwarded by afforced councils, great councils and parliaments. All in all, it is evident that both the king and his council were well informed of what was going on in Ireland. But in its day to day existence the council only infrequently discussed Irish affairs. A journal of the clerk of the council fortunately survives for 1392 and of the 43 sessions recorded, between January 1392 and February 1393, Irish business was discussed at only three, and then it was the proposed expedition of Gloucester to Ireland. Nor were any Irish notables, apart from the archbishop of Dublin, present at any session.

Nevertheless, at critical moments it was the council which took decisions and sent instructions to Ireland on what course of action was to be taken. On 24 June 1328, for example, the council debated the report of the 'dissensions commenced in the land of Ireland between the families (*linages*) of Geraldines and Poers' and the 'great perils' which would arise if a 'hasty remedy' was not provided. The decision was taken to send letters under the great seal ordering the feud to cease on pain of forfeiture. It was in council, too, that the conditions made by John Darcy for his appointment were discussed and decided on in August 1328. And it was in council on 2 October 1333 that many decisions were made regarding new appointments to office in Ireland.

Contact was maintained with Ireland in other ways, which must have kept the English government informed. Ever since the great reform of 1293, the Irish treasurer had to proceed at intervals to Westminster, to have his accounts audited by the barons of the exchequer. The long process of audit, frequently necessitating communication with Dublin, and the minute examination of records which covered much of the business of government, kept the English officials abreast of what was going on in Ireland. And since the king was the supreme dispenser of justice, which meant that his parliament was the final court of appeal, there was a regular stream of petitions from Ireland to England. The number grew enormously in the late thirteenth century, so that in the fourteenth century Irish petitions tended to be heard in council rather than in parliament. Council, therefore, became the main channel of communication.

There was one other link which was important, even though it was to be challenged in the fifteenth century. The principle that the king could legislate for Ireland was well established and therefore English statutes were regularly sent to Ireland to be proclaimed and enforced here. More that that, Irish business was often discussed in parliament – Irish magnates might be present – and the king occasionally legislated specifically for Ireland. As we have seen, it was in the English parliament of 1370 that the Irish problem of absentees was discussed, resulting in the Statute of Absentees. In 1323 and 1357 special ordinances *de statu terre Hibernie* ('concerning the state of the land of Ireland') were devised in England and sent to Dublin. Such legislation was usually in response to statements of grievance from

Ireland, when the business was too important to be dealt with in the day to day council.

Perhaps the most important business carried out in council in relation to Ireland was the appointment of a chief governor and the delegation to him of certain powers. If the theory seemingly was that acceptance of the office was obligatory, practice certainly allowed negotiation and bargaining before an appointment was taken up. A good illustration is the appointment of John Darcy as justiciar in 1328. He submitted a series of sixteen articles, outlining the conditions on which he was willing to go to Ireland. These are important, since they show what one man at least thought was necessary for good government in Ireland. Among other matters, he insisted on certain men being associated with him in office (obviously he distrusted some of the Dublin officials) and that he should have the right to supervise all offices. He also demanded the right to pardon for felony and that no Irish grants should be made without consulting him. But most interesting of all, he asked that all Irishmen wishing to live under English law be permitted by statute of the Irish parliament to do so, without having to buy a charter. Darcy clearly saw (what was maintained by Sir John Davies in the early seventeenth century) that the existence of two incompatible jurisdictions in Ireland made government difficult and at times impossible. The king and council told him to sound the opinion of the Irish magnates and in due course, in 1331, an ordinance was issued that there was to be one and the same law (*una et eadem lex*) for all Ireland.

Attempts at reform

But this attempt to give Gaelic Ireland the benefit of common law came decades too late and was largely ineffective. The gradual contraction of the land of peace continued and many disorders remained unchecked. Contact with England, at an unofficial level, helped to promote disorder in Ireland. The see-saw politics of England during the last decade or so of Edward II's reign had a marked effect on Ireland. The rise and fall of the Despensers and then Mortimer, reflected in Ireland not only by the mounting tension between the rival factions associated with le Poer and fitz Thomas, but also by the attempts of both sides to cash in on their control of the English government had a very unsettling effect. The descent of Robert Bruce on Ulster in 1327 created a panic: the Irish government informed the king of the 'frightful news' that Bruce proposed to conquer Ireland, though in fact he went back to Scotland soon after. It was the fall and execution of Mortimer in 1330 which helped restore some measure of stability. The new government in England took a hard look at Ireland and in 1331 issued a set of important ordinances which were intended to deal with the outstanding problems. The very first, for example, placed a severe limitation on the issuing of pardons. Others prescribed that there should be 'one and the same law' for Irish as well as English; that sheriffs and coroners were to be elected by the communities of the counties; hostages were to be kept in the royal castles only; truces between English and Irish were to be observed; royal castles were to be inspected every year; the justiciar was to 'cause inquiry every year concerning the officers of the lord the king . . . and punish delinquents'; private armies were not to be quartered on the countryside; all having lands in Ireland were to provide adequately for their defence. This was followed by an act resuming all grants made by the Mortimer regime, which threatened all his supporters in Ireland. Finally, it was announced that the king would visit Ireland to deal in person with remaining problems.

This more vigorous approach was maintained under a new justiciar, Sir Anthony Lucy, who tackled the problem of the rebellious earl of Desmond with ruthless efficiency. Preparations were well under way for the royal expedition to Ireland and it seemed that a real effort was about to be made to halt the seemingly inexorable process of disintegration which was undermining the settlement. But intervention in Scotland promised the young king better opportunities for glory and the Irish expedition was cancelled. This disastrous decision, followed shortly by the murder of the earl of Ulster which threw the whole of Ireland into confusion, was compounded when a large army (numbering over 1,500 men, of whom no less than 488 were men at arms) was withdrawn for service in the Scottish campaign of 1335. At a time when Ireland was in a desperate state, this was an irresponsible decision, especially since the cost of the expedition fell largely on the impoverished Irish exchequer. The O Mores, O Byrnes and O Briens were soon on the attack and in 1336 it was reported by Friar Clyn that all the Irish of Munster and Leinster had risen in war. A series of expeditions and parleys in the north, west and south did nothing to check the Gaelic lords. The Dublin government, corrupt as well as inefficient, was clearly in need of reform and drastic action was required. But despite complaints from some communities, nothing was done until 1341, when John Morice was sent to Dublin as deputy to the justiciar, with orders to carry out a great inquiry into the administration, including in particular an examination of the conduct of royal officials since 1330.

John Morice and the Anglo-Irish

A great revolution was now initiated. A fearsome order resumed all grants since the death of Edward I and Englishmen with property in England (and therefore capable of being distrained) were to be installed in office in Ireland. This naturally produced a fierce reaction in Ireland, since not only did it threaten the sinecures controlled by the powerful Anglo-Irish, but actually menaced their lands and titles as well. When a parliament, meeting in Dublin, was adjourned in the winter of 1341 it was reported that the

74

chief governor and his officials were afraid to attend. It was this parliament which drew up a series of petitions to the king, complaining bitterly of the conduct of the new government. The prior of the Hospital and Sir Thomas Wogan were chosen to travel to England and present the petitions to the king and his council. As it happens, the minutes of the council meeting which heard the petitions survive and they make it quite clear that a serious view was taken of the complaints.

A contemporary Anglo-Irish chronicle suggests that behind all this there was a deep resentment among the Anglo-Irish because of the attempted resumption and implying, too, resentment at the attempt to rule through Englishmen. Because of the resumption, the chronicler wrote, 'a great dispute arose in the land and the land of Ireland was on the point of separation from the lands of the king of England'. Referring to the Dublin parliament he wrote: '. . . before which time there never was such a notable and manifest division among the English born in England and the English born in Ireland'. Looking at the substance of their complaints as outlined in their petitions, we can clearly see signs of this anti-English spleen. They complain, for example, of 'those who are sent out of England to govern them, who themselves have little knowledge of your said land of Ireland, and have little or nothing at their coming there by which they can live and maintain their position, until they are supported by extortion under colour of their offices, to the great destruction of your people'. But it is hard to believe that this massive indictment of the government is all the result of Anglo-Irish resentment of the English, especially since so many of the charges ring true. The incompetence and corruption are highlighted and great stress is placed on the resulting lack of peace and order.

To all of this the king and council gave a sympathetic hearing. Almost every grievance was ordered to be redressed, which meant in effect the complete abandonment of the programme of reform initiated with the appointment of Morice. To further reassure the Anglo-Irish, the king dismissed the chancellor and appointed in his place the prior of the Hospital, one of the two messengers who had carried the petitions to England. Finally, early in 1344 Morice was dismissed and in July his replacement, Ralph of Ufford, arrived in Ireland. Yet another vigorous military regime was inaugurated and a new inquiry into the conduct of royal officials was ordered.

Ralph of Ufford and the continuing war

The new justiciar had a particular interest in Ireland, since he was married to the widow of the murdered earl of Ulster. The king must have hoped that not only would this act as an incentive to firm action in Ireland (where malicious gossip said that he was controlled by his wife), but that it would make him more acceptable to the Anglo-Irish lords. But to judge from the attitudes of the contemporary Dublin chronicler, Ufford alienated the locals: at his death, it was said, the bad weather which had lasted since first he arrived suddenly came to an end and the brighter weather enabled all to celebrate Easter in a truly joyful spirit! It may well be that the determination shown by Ufford in attacking the recalcitrant earl of Desmond and other rebel English shocked Anglo-Ireland. Writing to the king some months after his arrival, Ufford said that the land was just as much troubled by the English as it was by the Irish. Not only did he forge ahead relentlessly against Desmond, until the earl was forced to flee for his life and seek asylum in Gaelic Ireland, he also executed (in a horrible fashion and as a public example) some of his important adherents and threw the earl of Kildare into prison. Such firmness may have estranged the Anglo-Irish, but it was just what Ireland needed at that time. Unfortunately, however, Ufford died in April 1346 and once more the country lapsed into a state of disorder. When John Morice, the former justiciar, came to Ireland shortly afterwards, he reported to the king that the peace was disturbed. The appointment of Walter de Bermingham as justiciar, a member of one of the leading Anglo-Irish families, was clearly meant to assuage local feelings in the hope of restoring peace. To an extent the policy worked. During the next two years de Bermingham was able to use his local connexions to bring about a remarkable restoration of order, so that the machinery of government began to work with an efficiency not displayed for years. But all hope of continued progress was dashed in August 1348, when the great bubonic plague known as the Black Death reached Ireland and created havoc among the Anglo-Irish.

The Black Death in Ireland

The great plague, carried by rats and fleas, swept across Europe and reached the east coast of Ireland about early August 1348. It seems to have struck Drogheda first, though both Howth and Dalkey were later rivals for the doubtful privilege of being the ports of entry. It spread rapidly inland, hitting hardest the centres of population, where low standards of hygiene and poor sanitation encouraged the rats to breed. Friar Clyn of Kilkenny, himself a victim of the plague, has left a vivid account of its progress through the country. Within a few weeks both Dublin (where, he says, almost 14,000 people died before Christmas) and Drogheda were almost totally destroyed. 'This pestilence was so contagious, that those who touched the dead or persons sick of the plague were straightway infected themselves and died, so that the confessor and his penitent were carried to the same grave. And from very fear and horror men were seldom brave enough to perform the works of piety and mercy, such as visiting the sick and burying the dead. For many died from boils and ulcers and running sores which grew on the legs and beneath the armpits, whilst others suffered pains in the head and went almost into a frenzy, whilst others spat blood'. The mortality rate was terrific. Among the Franciscans, twenty-five died in their Drogheda house and twenty-three in Dublin. In Kilkenny, on 6 March 1349, eight of the Dominicans died. 'There was hardly a house in which one only had died', he wrote, 'but as a rule man and wife and their children and all the family went the common way of death'. People naturally panicked. The same flight from the towns to the countryside, so vividly described by Boccaccio in his *Decameron*, must have occurred here. Others flocked on pilgrimages to famous shrines. Clyn describes the thousands, 'prelates, nobles and others from divers parts of Ireland', wading into the river Barrow at St Mullins: 'Some came from the affection of devotion, but others (and they were the greater number) came from fear of the plague which was then at its greatest height'.

We can fitfully trace the spread of the plague from east to west, through Kilkenny (where, Clyn says, it was at its most virulent during the Lent of 1349) to Nenagh, where one Franciscan died on 10 August and another on 19 August 1349, to Limerick, where another Franciscan death was recorded shortly before 1 November 1349. The Irish annals confirm its presence in county Roscommon that same year: 'The great plague of the general pestilence that was throughout Ireland in Moy Lung this year, so that a great number of people died in it'.

It is impossible, of course, to estimate how many people died as a result of the plague. It recurred at intervals. There was another great outbreak in 1361 and regular references are made to it right down to the end of the middle ages. In England it is estimated that as many as 40 per cent of the population died as a result of the first outbreak and that by the end of the century the population may have been reduced by half. There is no reason to suppose that the mortality rate in Ireland, or at least in Anglo-Ireland, may have been appreciably lower. Archbishop Richard fitz Ralph believed it to be higher. He said that although the plague had not done much harm amongst the Irish, more than two-thirds of the English nation was wiped out. We cannot place much trust in the accuracy of fitz Ralph's estimate, though he was certainly voicing current opinion. So terrific were the losses that people commonly believed that the end of the world was near and that all would die. Friar Clyn gave voice to this fear when he wrote in his chronicle: 'Seeing these many ills and how the whole world is as it were in an ill plight, among the dead expecting death's coming I have set them down in writing, truthfully as I have heard them and tested them; and lest the writing should perish with the writer and the work fail with the worker, I leave parchment to carry on the work, if perchance any may survive or any of the race of Adam may be able to escape this pestilence and continue the work I have begun'. This was the last entry Clyn made in his chronicle. He died of the plague shortly after.

It seems certain that the plague was at its worst among the Anglo-Irish, in the towns and manors and other centres of population. This, as we have seen, was vouched for by Richard fitz Ralph. He also pointed out, what we might expect, that the plague fell more heavily on sailors, fishermen and those who lived near the sea. He argued before the pope in Avignon that on the occasion of the great jubilee year in 1350 the indulgence might be extended to those from Ireland without asking them to visit Rome. The effects of the plague were such, he said, that the council would never allow many to leave Ireland for fear that the depleted population would be the more easily exposed to attacks from the Irish enemies. And an official message from the Kilkenny great council of 1360, on the eve of the second great advent of plague in 1361, complained of 'the pestilence which is so great and so hideous among the English lieges and not among the Irish'.

It seems, therefore, that it was the Anglo-Irish communities which suffered most. The loss of a huge proportion of the population had catastrophic effects. Scarcity of labour necessitated the abandonment of manors; some boroughs were wiped out, to join the growing number of 'lost villages' in medieval Ireland; wages went spiralling upwards and prices naturally followed. The scarcity of skilled workers in England and the high wages attracted Irish artisans, accelerating the already alarming emigration rate. In the Church the results were disastrous, since many unsuitable people were recruited into the priesthood and the religious orders. The fear of death, the despair bred by the plague, which elsewhere in Europe led to the flagellants and other groups, can only have had a subversive effect. Already Ireland had been subjected to disorder and lawlessness on a growing scale. The Black Death and the recurrence of the plague greatly added to the general malaise of the age.

The crisis worsens

It was against this background that a new justiciar was appointed to Ireland. Sir Thomas Rokeby was a veteran soldier and it was clearly stated in his appointment that 'because the land of Ireland is not in good plight or in good peace', he was to bring a small force (20 men at arms and 40 mounted archers), in addition to his own retinue of 20 men at arms, 'the better to establish the peace of the land'. His primary function as chief governor, therefore, was to be a military one and, as we shall see, he did achieve a remarkable degree of success against the forces of disorder. During his first year in office, 1350, he was active in Leinster, as well as further afield in Munster. He enjoyed considerable success in Leinster, where he was able to achieve a settlement with the more important Gaelic lords in the mountains. What his achievements were in Munster and elsewhere is not very clear, though it is likely that Leinster was, necessarily, the focus of his attention at this time.

At the same time, Rokeby was active as an administrator. In the summer of 1350 he received instructions from the king ordering inquiries into various aspects of the administration and to force absentees to provide adequately for the defence of their lands. As a result, presumably, of Rokeby's inquiries, a set of orders was sent from England on 20 March 1351. These seem to show that there was no great need for any revolutionary overhaul of the Irish administration, since they deal with questions which can hardly be called critical: the fees of the marshal of the exchequer; the hearing of common pleas in the exchequer; the remuneration of exchequer clerks; the sale of lands and marriages in the king's hands. Only one of them was concerned with a question which affected the peace – an order to the justiciar 'not to grant any charter or pardon for felonies, especially those committed against Englishmen, without the assent and counsel of the chancellor and treasurer there, but to chastise disturbers of the peace and quiet of the land according to the law and custom thereof, since felons and other malefactors are thereby rendered bolder and the peace there is ill kept'. All of this suggests that a higher efficiency and probity was now reached in the administration than had been normal for generations past. It may well be, then, that Rokeby proved as efficient in civil affairs as in military and that he managed to clean up the Irish administration with remarkable success.

But this was either short-lived or illusory. A great council held in Kilkenny in November 1351 issued a series of ordinances which give a different view of the situation in Ireland. These ordinances are important because of their comprehensive character (there are 25 of them) and because they formed the basis subsequently for the definitive statutes of Kilkenny of 1366, which in many instances are word for word a repetition of Rokeby's ordinances. For that reason they repay close study. What is important in the first place is that the council was summoned 'upon the grievous complaints of the commons', so that the situation in the localities must have been far from good. This is reflected in the ordinances themselves. There is a prohibition against the quartering of private armies on the countryside (an old complaint) or the taking of victuals against an owner's will. There are many ordinances dealing with the problems of keeping the peace – concerning the pursuit of felons, the use of common law in place of 'the law of the march and the Brehon law', the problems of absentees, and the maintenance of robbers. Others dealt with defence – the conduct of parleys with the enemy, the principle of one war and one peace throughout Ireland, the imprisonment of English trucebreakers, the making of war by the English. The remainder dealt with purely administrative questions, such as the taking of sheriff's accounts, the fees of sheriffs, the duties of serjeants, the proclamation of the statute of labourers, and the fees of the marshals of the benches. At least 13 out of the 25 are concerned with the problems of defence and peace-keeping (which are hardly separable), so that this was obviously the burden of complaint from the localities and the question which weighed most with the administration.

After this Rokeby devoted himself again to his main task of pacification and with Leinster seemingly subjugated he concentrated on Munster. In 1353 he campaigned extensively there and once again he enjoyed an unusual degree of success. But once the pressure was removed, Leinster began to give trouble again and the justiciar was forced to lead new expeditions against the rebels late in 1353 (when he employed an army of more than 1,000 men), again in the autumn of 1354 (with over 1,100 men – the campaign ended in disaster), and yet again in the late spring of 1355. In addition, an extensive series of wards was established around the Wicklow mountains, though the government found it difficult to persuade magnates such as the earl of Kildare to fulfil their obligations in defending their marches. All of Rokeby's settlements were collapsing in 1355, possibly because he had overreached himself through an over-elaborate series of arrangements with a number of Gaelic lords. Lack of adequate finance, sufficient to sustain a network of wards, was certainly responsible in part. But as always, there was no successful way of keeping the pressure on the localities and forcing the Gaelic lords, or indeed the Anglo-Irish, to keep the terms agreed upon at submission. The principle of one war and one peace was impossible to maintain. The kind of balance of power which Rokeby had tried to achieve was not suited to the complicated politics of the Irish situation. The inevitable rebellions followed and in July 1355 Rokeby was replaced by the earl of Desmond, the former rebel.

The choice of Desmond shows some marks of desperation, since it was probably felt that only he could restore a measure of peace to Munster. But he died early in 1356 and between then and the appointment of the king's son, Lionel, as lieutenant in July 1361, no less than eight people held office as chief governor or deputy in Ireland. Nothing shows better how unstable the situation had become. Even the restoration of Rokeby in July 1356 (though he did not take up office until 31 December) did little to help. For although he again achieved a remarkable, though temporary, success in Leinster, he died on 23 April 1357 at Kilkea in county Kildare. His successors did little to retrieve a worsening situation, especially in Leinster where the Irish were federating. A Kilkenny parliament in January 1359 decided to send messengers 'to expound before the king and council arduous and urgent business concerning the land of Ireland'. But if the Dublin government hoped for help from England, it soon learnt that none would be forthcoming. Late in 1359, before his departure for France, Edward III announced that he was leaving England 'empty of armed power and destitute of lords, whereby there is no room to send men or money to Ireland at present, although it is said that they are needed there'.

It was time to inform the king of the realities of the situation in Ireland. A great council met at Kilkenny in July 1360 and sent an urgent message to the king. It complained bitterly of the failure of absentees, 'who own the fifth part of the said land and more', to defend their lands (the king's son Lionel being one of those and others being his confidants); it bemoaned the lack of lords, partly the result of the Black Death, who might defend the localities, where the lieges are so enfeebled that they can no longer defend themselves; and it decried the impoverishment of the lieges 'by divers oppressions, without payments made, tallages, and bad government of former ministers' as well as 'fervent and continual wars'. The treasury is empty, so that war cannot be maintained or the land defended. 'The Irish, your enemies, of one assent and covenant, commence to levy war throughout all your land, burning, destroying and preying daily your lieges of those parts', growing in strength and conquering 'a great part of the land in divers marches'. Unless succour and relief is sent in all haste from England, they will (God forbid) conquer the whole land. In the end, because they 'can no longer endure', they ask the king 'as a work of charity' to send to their relief out of England 'a good sufficient chieftain, stocked and strengthened with men and treasure, of which they can live . . . as a noble and gracious prince is bound to do for his lieges'.

This must have shocked the king and before the year was out he had decided to send his son Lionel, earl of Ulster and shortly afterwards duke of Clarence, to Ireland at the head of the largest army sent here since King John came in 1210. It marks a new departure. Up to this time the chief governor, though he may have brought a small force with him (as Rokeby did) in addition to his own retinue of 20, had to work within the military resources of the lordship. The intervention of Edward III through Clarence marks the beginning of a massive military and financial investment in Ireland, which had as its object the restoration of order and, if possible, the recovery of lost lands.

4   The Attempt at Recovery

The financial problem of Ireland

In 1366 Edward III addressed a parliament which had been
critical of the high cost of the Irish wars, where the king's
son had been at war in an attempt to answer a cry for help
from the Dublin government. In his speech the king made it
plain that not only did he now expect to make Ireland pay
her own way again, but he hoped to recoup his investment
by drawing on a surplus revenue. He spoke of Ireland as a
place which 'had been profitable' and that his son was there
'in hope that it should be so again in the future'. That this
was an idle hope is easy to demonstrate. But it is a fact that
in the second half of the fourteenth century it seems to have
been a constant hope of English governments that there
might be a return to the halcyon days of the thirteenth
century, when far from being a financial liability, Ireland
had been a lucrative source of revenue. Writing of Richard
II's first expedition to Ireland, the English chronicler
Walsingham pointed out that in the time of Edward III,
£30,000 a year came from Ireland, but that nothing came
from there now. Walsingham, of course, is hopelessly
inaccurate; but he does reflect opinion in contemporary
England that in the not too remote past Ireland had been a
source of great profit to the Crown. Richard II certainly
retained hopes of making it so again. When de Vere was
granted Ireland in 1385 and 1386, it was on condition that
after the conquest of Ireland he was to pay 5,000 marks
annually into the English exchequer. Gloucester, in his

indenture of 1392, agreed that after three years Ireland would be self-supporting and money from England should cease.

But such hopes were wholly unrealistic. The English government continued to lay out large sums of money on Ireland throughout the second half of the fourteenth century. Thousands of pounds were spent on the armies sent with Clarence, Windsor, Gloucester and, of course, on the great expeditions led by Richard II to Ireland in the last years of the century. The English taxpayer continued to pay out, with no sign of any real return on the expenditure. In fact, the English government overreached itself financially and many Irish chief governors were left well short of the sums promised in their contracts for service. When Mortimer, for example, was appointed chief governor in 1379, his agreed stipend was 20,000 marks. But when he died suddenly in 1381, his pay was already 10,000 marks in arrears. The trouble was that the English government itself was frequently short of money and could ill afford expenditure on Ireland.

Edward III made no secret of the fact that, as he put it in one of his letters, 'neither the king nor his subjects of England can comfortably bear these expenses . . . upon the upkeep of the war in Ireland'. The real burden of his complaint was that these expenses had been incurred in Ireland 'without taking any revenues or profits therefrom'. So, when he and his successor, Richard II, continued to pour money into the Irish wars, it can only be because they hoped to at least make Ireland self-sufficient again and, hopefully, a source of profit. This could only be achieved by restoring the rule of law, extending the hand of peace, and revitalising the traditional sources of revenue in the lordship. Even taxation, however heavy its incidence, was not going to be very lucrative until the area of taxable land was increased. All of this meant a recovery of lost land, partly through reconquest, partly through forcing absentees to reoccupy estates, and possibly through a new colonisation of waste and depopulated lands (this was a condition of service demanded by the duke of Surrey at the end of the century, when he was appointed chief governor of Ireland). Inevitably it involved the government in war, which the English taxpayer had to support. Naturally, too, heavy expenditure on war must be more immediately controlled from England, so that investments were generally made through English chief governors (usually with military experience), who would get the maximum return from Ireland. This policy of direct intervention from England, with the aim of making some recovery in Ireland, was initiated when the king's son Lionel was sent as chief governor to Ireland at the head of any army and supported out of the English exchequer.

Clarence in Ireland

Prince Lionel had Irish connexions through his wife, the heiress of the last earl of Ulster. Lionel now held that title, and was soon made duke of Clarence. Long before this, in the previous decade, there had been a serious proposal to send him to Ireland, where his estates were steadily slipping from his grasp. Nothing came of the proposal and the general situation in Ireland, especially in the north and west where Lionel's lands lay, gradually worsened. The appeal for help from the Irish council in July 1360 could not be left unanswered and the happy coincidence that a truce had been negotiated with France in May, followed later by the treaty of Brétigny which brought the war to an end, left the king with resources to spare for Ireland. There was also a long truce with Scotland. A large-scale intervention was thus possible and it was an opportune time for Lionel to see to his responsibilities in Ireland. In March 1361 the king announced that 'we have for the salvation of the said land ordained that our dear son Lionel shall proceed thither with all dispatch and with a great army'.

In making this announcement, Edward stressed 'the impotence of our lieges' in Ireland, which enabled the Irish enemies to subject the land 'to such devastation and destruction that, unless God avert and succour the same it will be plunged soon into total ruin'. But he laid equal blame on 'the magnates of our land of England having land there (who) take the profits thereof but do not defend them'. No fewer than 64 of these absentees were now summoned to Westminster, not only to advise the king's son, but to accompany him to Ireland in person or by proxy. Later, in July, a royal ordinance ordered all with lands in Ireland to defend them or risk confiscation. That this was no idle threat was realised later when Clarence did confiscate lands which he had conquered.

In preparation for the expedition elaborate arrangements were made to supply the duke with an adequate army, a substantial war chest and a fleet. John of Clifton spent £400 on shipping in Liverpool and Chester. Twenty-two ships, many of them Irish, were pressed into service to carry Clarence and his contingent. The flagship was specially fitted out, in accordance with the duke's own directions. Four sconces and ten round lanterns were bought on his instructions. Different coloured worsteds were used as hangings and a blue carpet was purchased for his own cabin. Like so many medieval travellers, Clarence sailed under the protection of St Christopher and John of Clifton accounted for the making of an image of the saint 'for a safe voyage'. Material was also bought to make a great star, fixed to the sail, which was the emblem under which the duke sailed to Ireland.

The army which he brought with him was not especially large, though it was to cost the English exchequer a great sum of money to maintain. The accounts of the clerk of the wages, Walter of Dalby, have fortunately survived and they show that altogether the different contingents came to around 900 men. There was a high proportion of men at arms and the rest were mounted archers. It is obvious that the infantry, usually the most numerous of the troops, were to be recruited in Ireland. The largest contingent was led by the earl of Stafford, an experienced veteran who was the real commander-in-chief of the army. After landing in Ireland he recruited an O Kennedy to augment his force. and this must have been what other leaders did as well. O Kennedy served against the Irish of Leinster for a total of 156 days (with a break of ten days for Christmas) with a troop of 11 hobelars (at 4d. a day each) and 88 foot (at 1½d. each), rates which fell short of those current at the time. He himself was paid 12d. a day. Some of the Anglo-Irish, such as the earl of Ormond, also served with contingents in some campaigns.

But any hope the English had of greatly augmenting the army through recruitment in Ireland was destroyed by the spleen which existed between the local Anglo-Irish and those who came over from England. We have already seen evidence from the previous decade of Anglo-Irish resentment of English interference in Ireland. There is evidence that this resentment continued to boil over. The king referred to it in the summer of 1364: 'divers dissensions and debates [had] arisen between the English born in England and the English born in Ireland his subjects, whereby in times past hurt and peril has happened in Ireland, and worse is feared unless the same be speedily appeased'. A Dublin chronicler reported that Clarence himself, shortly after arriving and while preparing to campaign in Wicklow, issued a proclamation that no person born in Ireland should come near his camp, and that this was made an excuse to kill 100 of his soldiers. Clarence might have issued such an order, aware of the animosity between the two peoples. But even if the story is entirely apocryphal, the chronicler certainly reflects the bitter distrust of one for the other. In 1366 the famous statutes of Kilkenny dealt with the problem in a forthright way, by stipulating 'that no difference of allegiance henceforth be made between the English born in Ireland and the English born in England by calling them *English hobbe* and *Irish dog*, but that all shall be called by one name, the English lieges of our lord the king'. It is very likely, too, that the duke's plan of reconquest frightened those Anglo-Irish who had usurped the lands of absentees in Leinster.

It is not easy to discover exactly what Clarence and his army did in Ireland. There was certainly a campaign in Wicklow shortly after his arrival and campaigns later in Munster and Leinster. But the details escape us. The duke was obviously not expecting to be exclusively occupied in war, since elaborate preparations were made to entertain himself and his entourage before his arrival in Dublin. After he took up residence in the castle, further works 'for his games and pleasure' were ordered. The gardens were improved and a barge built at the request of his wife. Provision was also made for the holding of tournaments within the castle grounds. So, a splendid court was set up and military matters were not allowed to dominate the life of the duke. One suspects that he left the conduct of campaigns to the seasoned veteran, Stafford, but this cannot be proved.

Whatever the court was doing in Dublin, the army certainly saw action. Walter of Dalby, the clerk of the wages, paid out sums of money as compensation to the owners of horses lost on campaign. *The Annals of the Four Masters* record that in 1362 Art Mac Murrough, the king of Leinster, and his heir Donal, were taken prisoners. Froissart later described a campaign in Leinster and a battle in which 'many were slain and taken on both sides'. The king, in a letter in February 1362, ordered the absentees to Ireland, where his son 'and the lieges with him are in peril from the increasing strength of the said [Irish] enemies', because the English had lost so many men. This might have been partly the result of a new and virulent outbreak of the plague in 1361; but it must also have been the result of action against the Irish. There was activity in the north, too, since O Neill apparently did homage. And in Munster, where O Brien of Thomond also did homage, there is evidence of the recovery of much land in Cork, 'which had long been wasted by the Irish of the parts of Munster, enemies of the king, and which were perambulated by the king's lieutenant with a great army and by great war acquired'. There was also a campaign, late in 1362, against the O Connors, who had raided into Meath. Early in 1364 there was a campaign in Leix and yet another one into the Wicklow mountains.

It is impossible to discern any pattern in all this military activity. But it is very likely that Clarence and his council were worried about the increasing Gaelic pressure, from east and west, on the river systems of Leinster, and in particular on the Barrow, which was the main line of communication between north and south Leinster. This was the most densely populated area and the most prosperous. It had to be protected. For this reason Clarence took a revolutionary decision, to move the exchequer and the common bench to Carlow and thus make it the administrative centre of the lordship. The decision was made early (it may even have been taken in England), for in October 1361 the sheriff of Dublin was finding carts to transport the exchequer to Carlow. The great castle there was repaired, as were the town walls.

Carlow had the advantage of easy access, being much closer than Dublin to the heart of the lordship. It was in a commanding position on the Barrow and was ideally placed for campaigns into the mountains, or westwards into the marches of Leix and Offaly. In theory, therefore, it was an ideal choice as the capital of the lordship. But by now, in fact, Carlow was dangerously close to the independent Gaelic enclaves which had been causing such concern to the government. In 1364 the treasurer complained that because the exchequer at Carlow was 'on the frontier of the Irish rebels, there is no safe access to it by the king's lieges'. There were constant complaints. Exchequer officials were outraged by the high prices charged for food and later complained that they lived in danger of their lives. Accountants refused to present themselves in Carlow because of the danger. Others, such as the mayors of Waterford or Cork, had to be excused coming to take their oaths of office 'because of the danger of the way'. The town was attacked, houses were burned, records were lost. There was a trickle of refugees abandoning the town for safer parts, until by the later fourteenth century the situation was desperate. Finally, when Richard II came on his first expedition he decided that Carlow was no longer suitable as an administrative centre and shifted the exchequer back to Dublin.

An interesting experiment therefore failed in the end. The military side of Clarence's rule fared no better. By April 1364 it was clear that the forces he had in Ireland were insufficient for any worthwhile recovery of land. The duke therefore decided to return to England for reinforcements. Already the clerk of the wages had paid out over £22,000, and for this huge outlay little of worth had been achieved. It was a chastened Clarence who sailed from Ireland on 25 April. He left Ormond behind as deputy, with only the rump of the army – 6 knights, 60 squires and 60 mounted archers. When he returned in December he brought another army with him. Numbers are not known; but to judge from the extensive search made for adequate shipping to transport the army to Ireland, it must have been considerably larger than that which came in 1361. William Spaldyng arrested ships in a great sweeping arc from Southampton to Bristol, all over Severn water and on to Chester and Furness. He carried out a special arrest for William of Windsor, especially in the Welsh ports and in Chester and Liverpool. At any rate, Clarence seems to have taken the field again after he came back to Ireland, especially in the south. But things must have gone badly for him, at least at first, since the king wrote in February 1365 that Ireland was 'sunk in the greatest wretchedness'. Clarence certainly moved around the country during that year, but his achievements (if any) remain a mystery. Then suddenly he summoned a parliament to meet at Kilkenny in the spring of 1366 and this produced the body of statutes with which his name is always linked and which has been taken as his only solid achievement in Ireland.

The statutes of Kilkenny

Lionel's purpose in summoning this parliament is well set-out in the preamble to the legislation which it enacted and is worth quoting at length. 'Whereas at the conquest of the land of Ireland and for a long time after, the English of the said land used the English language, mode of riding and apparel and were governed and ruled, they and their subjects called *Betaghes*, by the English law; in which time the rights of God and of the Holy Church and their liberties according to their conditions were maintained in due obedience. But now many English of the said land, forsaking the English language, fashion, mode of riding, laws and usages, live and govern themselves according to the manners, fashion and language of the Irish enemies, and also have made divers marriages and alliances between themselves and the Irish enemies aforesaid; whereby the said land and the liege people thereof, the English language, the allegiance due to our lord the King, and the English laws there are put in subjection and decayed and the Irish enemies exalted and raised up contrary to right'.

The problem of degeneracy therefore was uppermost and there is a group of statutes which tries to govern relations between the two communities. They forbid alliance by marriage, fosterage or concubinage; the presentation of Irishmen to cathedral or collegiate churches; the reception of Irish minstrels and other entertainers amongst the English; the acceptance of Irishmen into profession in English religious houses; the use of the Irish language, mode of riding and dress; the giving of pasturage on lands to Irish (a significant indication of how the Irish were continually pressing in on the land of peace).

None of the above statutes (save that dealing with alliances) was based on the ordinances of 1351, which is an indication that the parliament of 1366 regarded the problems they dealt with as fairly novel. But most of the remaining statutes are borrowed from the 1351 ordinances and are simply providing traditional remedies for longstanding problems. Here again the preamble is informative. After describing how parliament met on 18 February, it says that the legislation agreed to was 'for the good governance of the said land and quiet of the people and for the better observance of the laws and the punishment of evil doers'. Many of the statutes attempt to regulate war with the Irish (including the notorious one which forbids, in the marches, 'the games which men call "hurlings" with great clubs at ball upon the ground, from which great evils and maims have arisen to the weakening of the defence of the said land'); others deal with the maintenance of order in the land of peace; some safeguard the rights and liberties of the Church; a very important, and neglected, group are concerned with the fees and conduct of royal officials (in February 1363 the king had ordered an inquiry into the conduct of his officials in Ireland); another group deals with the administration of the law; and two most interesting ones attempt to fix wages and prices.

Succeeding generations gave a status to this corpus of statutes far beyond that accorded to any other similar body of legislation in the middle ages. It is easy to see why. Although very little of it was new, it did codify the most important parts of existing legislation which dealt with current problems and this was done in the presence of the king's son. But this does not mean that the statutes mark any new departure. They did not amount to 'a real out-lawry of the *mere* Irish', as Edmund Curtis once suggested. Nor do they show any sign of the abandonment of 'a long attempt to conquer the whole island', so that 'the government decided to keep what it could of the country'. It was not in the nature of a king such as Edward III to abandon any part of his patrimony and both he and Richard II spent large sums of money trying to extend the area in which royal writs were effective.

After the successful conclusion of his parliament, Lionel campaigned again in Munster and seems to have succeeded in reconquering some land. He returned to Dublin in the autumn and on 7 November he left for home. The death of his wife in 1363 (which might have been one reason why he went back to England in the spring of 1364) had broken his connexion with Ireland and he was obviously not anxious to stay. Nor can it be said in truth that his achievements were such that there was any clamour to retain him. Something had been gained. For one thing, there was some improvement in the financial situation. During the period 21 April 1359 to 11 February 1360, the Irish treasurer accounted for a total of £2,227. But from 14 January 1362 to 9 April 1364 it rose to £6,203. And from 1 February 1365 to 28 July 1366 it came to £4,250. But this hardly justified the massive expenditure incurred by the expeditions. Militarily, too, the lieutenancy of Clarence was not a great success. Whatever he achieved, and it is doubtful if that amounted to very much, was soon swept away. Even the choice of Carlow as capital was not a success. Only a few months after the departure of Clarence, a parliament complained to the king that both the Irish enemies and others (presumably rebels) 'rode in hostile array through every part of the said land, committing homicides, robberies and arsons, pillaging, spoiling and destroying monasteries, churches, castles, towns and fortresses' and prophesying that 'the land was at point to be lost, if remedy and help were not immediately supplied'. Even allowing for an inordinate degree of exaggeration, this petition clearly shows that Clarence's mission of pacification had been a complete failure.

William of Windsor in Ireland

To make matters worse, the war with France was renewed at the end of 1369, which naturally meant that there was not going to be much to spare for Ireland. New legislation against absentees did nothing to help – indeed it has recently been shown that this had the effect of persuading a number of the more important to pull out of Ireland and to sell their manors to Anglo-Irish magnates resident there. But before the king had become committed to the French war again, he had appointed William of Windsor as lieutenant of Ireland and showed that he was prepared to continue his heavy investment in Ireland.

Windsor had a soldier's experience of Ireland, since he was in the company of Clarence during the latter's expedition, serving with a large contingent of 60 men at arms and 66 archers. He had, therefore, some knowledge of Irish problems before he was appointed lieutenant of the king. His service as keeper of Carlisle not only gave him valuable experience of border warfare, but also an intimate knowledge of the problems of existence in a frontier area. He was well suited to govern Ireland. His indenture of 1 February 1369 stipulated that he was to bring with him 200 men at arms and 300 mounted archers, reducing to 120 and 200 during his second year in office, and 80 and 150 during his third. Nor was there to be any cut-back in the subsidies from England; Windsor was to receive £10,000 during his first year, £6,000 during his second, and £4,000 during his third. In fact, he brought an extra 50 men at arms and 60 archers and therefore received an additional £2,300. From 20 June 1369 (the day he arrived in Dublin) until 20

June 1372 (when he was back in England), the English exchequer paid out more than £22,000 in support of Windsor's campaigns in Ireland.

It is quite clear from the figures agreed to in the contract between Windsor and the king that there was to be a steady reduction in England's military and financial involvement in Ireland. This necessarily meant that the new lieutenant was expected to find adequate resources in Ireland, both in men and money, to help support the wars there. He did not fail in this. The enrolled account of the Irish treasurer, the bishop of Meath, for the period 17 July 1368 to 2 September 1372, shows payments of nearly £8,000 to the clerks of the wages in charge of the financing of Windsor's campaigns. And it is almost certain that an additional £2,855, from two subsidies granted to the lieutenant, also went on wages of war. So that during the period of less than three years which he spent in Ireland, Windsor paid out nearly £33,000 to his troops. War, then, was his primary concern.

It is significant that a Dublin chronicler characterises him as 'a vigorous and spirited knight in arms', for this is how he must have been remembered. Like so many chief governors before him, he found himself immediately involved with the Irish of the mountains south of Dublin. He engaged in sporadic war in the mountains until the summer of 1370, and with some success since the ruling Mac Murrough was captured and executed. But the lieutenant was diverted to Munster, where O Brien and Mac Namara of Thomond had led a great rising, imprisoning some of the leading Anglo-Irish (including the earl of Desmond) and killing others. They also burnt Limerick. Windsor's Munster campaign is not well documented, so there is considerable doubt about his activity there. His enemies later accused him of spending 22 weeks at Adare without going to war. But whatever truth there may be in that, he at least succeeded in procuring submissions from both O Brien and Mac Namara before the end of 1370.

So far, then, he had been successful in Leinster and Munster. The new year saw him engaging O Kennedy of Ormond. But the sustained war was taking its toll. Windsor could only continue by procuring lavish parliamentary subsidies. This he did, using force when he had to. There was a natural reaction and complaints began to reach the king about his high-handed behaviour. In 1371, too, there was another violent outbreak of the plague, which exacerbated an already difficult situation. In the latter part of the year the king began to take a hand, ordering suspension of disputed taxes and finally ordering Windsor back to England. On 20 March he left Ireland, in disgrace, having been subjected to a series of humiliating restrictions during his last weeks in office.

There seems to have been an immediate reaction in Munster, where O Brien renewed the war. There are obvious signs of panic in government circles in April 1372, when (as a meeting of the council in Dublin was told) Mac Namara, Richard Óg de Burgh of Connacht and 'almost all the Irish of Munster, Connacht, and Leinster, and many English, rebels and enemies, had risen openly to war after the departure of William of Windsor, lieutenant of the king in Ireland, and had confederated to make a universal conquest of the whole of Ireland before the same lieutenant should come from England'. There was a series of afforced councils at Dublin, Drogheda, Trim and Naas, to discuss the perilous conditions which had developed after Windsor's departure. An order to the mayor of Drogheda, informing him of the council to be held there on 7 April and instructing him to have the burgesses present, contains the curious mandate that he should not permit any men at arms of the retinue of Windsor 'to leave through the gate of the town'. There is other evidence that Windsor's army was trying to follow him out of Ireland, which would have left the government without professional troops to send against the rebels.

99

Windsor's replacement was Robert Ashton, a former chancellor, who sealed an indenture with the king on 8 March 1372, contracting to bring a force of 60 men at arms and 100 mounted archers from England, with an extra 80 hobelars and 200 foot which he was to raise in Ireland. He got off to a bad start, for when his English troops were arrayed after his arrival, four of his men at arms and six of the archers were found to be Anglo-Irish. Ashton, therefore, had defaulted on his contract. The locals were not satisfied with him and a parliament in January 1373 requested that he be replaced. The king was finding it difficult to get anyone to take on the rule of Ireland. Windsor had been cleared of the accusations against him and great pressure was now brought on him to take office in Ireland again. He was naturally reluctant to do so and made firm conditions (such as the payment of disputed subsidies) before finally agreeing to serve. On 20 September 1373, he sealed his new indenture as 'governor and keeper', contracting to bring 200 men at arms and 400 archers for £11,213.6.8. But it wasn't until 18 April 1374 that he landed in Waterford.

Again, it is difficult to follow Windsor's movements exactly. Evidence taken at inquisitions later accused him of ignoring the war in Munster, despite appeals for help. Even as late as 1378, when further evidence was collected in inquisitions taken at Dublin, the accusation was levelled against him that having come to Dublin in April 1374 he stayed there for seventeen weeks, with the O Byrnes waging war in Leinster. Windsor, having gone into the castle 'with all his company', reputedly 'said openly that if the whole country of the king were being burnt, he would not arm against the Irish enemies until the tallage granted to him at Kilkenny and Balidoill were paid'. These disputed subsidies were a sore point with everybody and the lack of payment may have caused Windsor to hesitate before getting involved in expensive military operations. He managed to keep Leinster under surveillance, while helping to keep alive a war between O Brien and Mac Namara in Munster. He even succeeded in persuading a Kilkenny parliament in June 1375 to grant a subsidy, even though it was only the ludicrously low sum of 400 marks.

But by now relations between Windsor and the Anglo-Irish had reached such a low point that not even the reports of widespread war in Munster, Connacht and Leinster could move them to make adequate grants of money to the government. The poor financial state of the exchequer is revealed in the account of John Colton, treasurer of Ireland, for the period 6 May 1372 to 30 September 1375, which records receipt of only £6,239, and payments of only £2,053 to clerks of the wages. Clearly there was no hope of the Irish exchequer becoming financially independent of England once more. The king tried pressurising the Irish parliament, sending Nicholas Dagworth as his special ambassador to address parliament at Kilkenny and expound the great need of financial support. But parliament refused to be moved and Dagworth then revealed the king's demand that all the local communities should send representatives to a special meeting in England, where he hoped that a subsidy might be granted. This, as we shall see, produced a terrific reaction and a constitutional crisis of unprecedented proportions developed.

Windsor was still in serious financial difficulties and his soldiers were beginning to desert for want of pay. It was impossible to pursue any kind of consistent policy, not knowing where the next penny was to come from. The whole situation was made worse when Windsor and the Irish government became the focus of attack by the resistance movement in England to the inner circle of favourites and financiers who dominated the king, prominent among them being Alice Perrers, the wife of the lieutenant. The resistance was led by Edmund Mortimer, who was able to use his widespread Irish connexions to secure a growing

volume of complaint against Windsor and his administration. Serious charges were concocted against them and
the chief royal officials were dismissed. Windsor himself
had to come before the council to answer these charges, but
late in 1376 all proceedings against him were dropped.

Windsor and the Irish parliament

It is easy to show that many of the charges against the
government are wildly exaggerated, even if they did contain a measure of truth. The real source of bitterness, on
both sides, was the necessity to make Ireland increasingly
responsible for the cost of her wars. This meant that
Windsor had to procure subsidies on an unprecedented
scale and it was his efforts to do this, and the methods which
he applied, that caused the constitutional crisis which was
to remove him from office. He summoned a large number
of representative assemblies (four parliaments and four
councils during his first term in office, and three parliaments
and one council during his second term). In each of these
twelve assemblies, held in the short space of less than five
years, he requested a subsidy of some kind. The opposition
from the commons grew. They complained of their losses
in the wars, their poverty, and the heavy burden of taxation. According to the evidence produced later, Windsor
refused to accept this argument and through different kinds
of pressure forced consent from the commons. For example,
the commons of county Meath said that on 8 June 1371 a
parliament was held at Ballyduagh, a waste place where
there was no suitable housing available for their elected
representatives and where no provision had been made to
feed them. After resisting Windsor's demands for three
days, they were worn out by their stay in that place and
they capitulated. But their consent was not freely given.
The county of Louth complained that its representatives
were thrown into prison by an angry Windsor at another

parliament where they refused to agree to his request for a subsidy. These are typical of complaints made by the commons of other shires and towns. They gave their consent 'because of the extortion of the lieutenant' and the subsidies were levied 'against the will of the community of the county' or 'against their will by extortion'.

This argument raised the whole question of elected representatives and their power. It clarified the important principle that communities were bound by the assent of their elected representatives in parliament. But such consent must be freely given, otherwise it could not be binding. The demand of the king in 1376 that the local communities should send elected representatives to a council meeting in England raised a further important question: could the commons be compelled to send representatives outside Ireland? When Nicholas Dagworth produced his writs of summons, the matter was hotly debated. During the elections which followed, the local communities stoutly declared they were under no obligation to answer the summonses and send representatives to England. But because of the state of Ireland and the gravity of the situation there, and out of reverence for the king, they were willing on this occasion, and of their own free will and saving their liberties, to accede to the request of the king. They refused, however, to give their elected representatives full power to consent to a subsidy, thus defeating the whole purpose of the meeting.

This open defiance must have astonished Windsor. He again attempted to force the communities into surrender. In the case of Dublin, he found an excuse to order a new election in November, one of his reasons being the refusal of the electors to grant the power of consenting to taxation. He appointed the treasurer and the chief justice of the bench to supervise the new election, making sure that the power of consent was granted this time. But despite the threat of being 'distrained by all their lands and chattels', and the presence of the two royal officials, the electors still withheld full power of consent to taxation.

The king contracts out of Ireland

The failure of William of Windsor meant the end of Edward III's expressed hopes of recovering his financial investment in Ireland. But the king continued to pay armies going to Ireland. Ormond was appointed chief governor, sealing an indenture in August 1376 and agreeing to bring a force of 120 men at arms and 200 archers to Ireland. He arrived on 4 October and between then and 4 October 1377 there is a recorded expenditure of over £5,000 on his troops. Edward III, however, died in June 1377 and his successor, Richard II, was a minor. The English council seemed reluctant to spend money on Ireland and the military situation there deteriorated rapidly. Ormond incurred much expense in trying to keep troops in the field and it wasn't until August 1379 that he succeeded in getting the English council to make provision for the payment of his debts. Then on 22 October Edmund Mortimer, who as well as being earl of March was lord of Meath, earl of Ulster and lord of Connacht in Ireland, was appointed lieutenant in Ireland. It is significant that in addition to getting 20,000 marks from England, Mortimer was given the revenues of Ireland without being accountable for them.

This marks a radical departure. We have seen the growing practice in the fourteenth century for chief governors to be appointed under contract. Elaborate indentures were sealed mutually, setting out the terms of service – mainly the period of service, the forces to be brought to Ireland, the stipend to be paid, and the powers to be enjoyed by the new chief governor. These contracts were binding on both parties. We have seen, for example, that some of Ashton's troops were disallowed on array, because they were not English as was stipulated in his indenture. The English parliament agreed to pay Sir Philip Courtenay a substantial sum of money as compensation for losses suffered when the king broke his contract with him as lieutenant of Ireland. On 20 October 1371, the king invoked his indenture against William of Windsor, pointing out that this indenture laid down the conditions governing Windsor's appointment and that he had now gone beyond the limits thus imposed on his government.

But when Mortimer was exempted from accounting for the revenues of Ireland a major step was taken by the king in contracting out of the governance of Ireland. It was an arrangement that could have worked to the advantage of both parties only if Ireland could produce sufficient revenue to free the king from the financial burden and to enable the chief governor to provide adequate rule. And for a time, there does seem to have been some sign of recovery after the series of interventions which began with the appointment of Clarence in 1361. It has recently been shown, from the surviving exchequer records for the period 1388 to 1391, that receipts were coming in regularly from Dublin, Kilkenny, Wexford, Limerick, Meath and Louth; and that some revenue was coming from Carlow, Cork and Tipperary. But there still was nothing like enough money even to enable the Irish government to pay its officials regularly. Ormond, as we saw, was appointed justiciar in July 1376. His stipend, to be paid out of the Irish exchequer, was the traditional one of £500 a year. But by February 1379 his arrears had come to nearly £370. Because there was 'nothing in the king's treasury of Ireland wherewith to pay the said sums', the king agreed to pay him the arrears. So, investment from England continued: Mortimer, as we saw, was promised 20,000 marks in 1379; Gloucester in 1392 was granted 34,000 marks; and in 1398 Surrey was promised 11,500 marks a year. Internally, too, every chief governor was still dependent on the good will and cooperation of the Anglo-Irish magnates, who were still an essential element in the governance of the lordship. This was well demonstrated when the earl of Ormond died in 1382. The bishop of Ossory reported that 'the whole land of Munster, together with a great part of Leinster, is desolated and endangered, and the Irish enemies and our English rebels of those parts, who formerly were accustomed to be ruled and subjected by the earl, now rise to war against our lieges there'.

The greatest example of the attempt to govern Ireland through contract was the grant to Robert de Vere in 1385. The king announced on 12 October that he was going to bestow the title of marquis of Dublin on his great favourite, de Vere. On 1 December he was granted the land of Ireland for life, with writs running his name and his arms replacing those of the king. It was widely believed in England at the time that there was a more sinister purpose behind all this, namely to develop Ireland as a power base, in association with Cheshire and Wales. But there is no doubt that in addition to providing for his favourite, the king was trying to free himself of the burden of Ireland. While de Vere was given lavish grants to maintain the huge force of 500 men at arms and 1,000 archers for two years, it was anticipated that a programme of reconquest would make Ireland once more a source of profit. Hence de Vere's grant was conditional on his paying 5,000 marks a year for Ireland in the future. De Vere's grant more or less made Ireland a palatinate for him. But he never came to Ireland and when he suffered exile and forfeiture as a result of political change in England, his grant lapsed. His successor, Sir John Stanley, was appointed on more normal terms, with a retinue of 100 men at arms and 400 archers and a stipend of 8,000 marks a year.

A deteriorating situation in Ireland

All this provided no answer to the problems of Ireland. A new menace was the increased tendency of the Gaelic lords to confederate, not only in Leinster but in Munster as well. In desperation, the government was trying to buy off the more threatening lords, such as Mac Murrough and O Brien. But given the desperate financial position of the government, there was no hope of permanently compensating the Gaelic chieftains. Shortly after his appointment in 1379 Mortimer had to lend the king £1,000 to help defray the cost of his expedition to Ireland. When he suddenly died on the night after Christmas in 1381, both Desmond and Ormond refused to take charge of the government, such was the financial risk involved. When the council brought great pressure to bear on John Colton, he reluctantly agreed to take the office, but only on condition that he be allowed to relinquish it in the next parliament. The appointment of an English nonentity, Sir Philip Courtenay, was hardly calculated to reassure those in Ireland who felt that a strong intervention from England was urgently needed. Courtenay encountered very considerable hostility and in the summer of 1385, while he was away campaigning in Leinster, a meeting of the council in Kilkenny criticised him and asked the king that he himself should come to Ireland, or at least send one of his great magnates. This request was repeated at a great council in Dublin in October.

The appointment of de Vere was the king's answer, followed by that of Sir John Stanley (who had, in fact, been acting as de Vere's deputy in Ireland). On the whole, Stanley's period in office was a disaster. The capture of the son of the reigning O Neill, Niall Óg, gave him a great advantage in Ulster. But he muffed it, releasing Niall after a few months. This news was badly received by Richard II, but it was too late for him to intervene. The advantage had been lost and Gaelic Ulster increasingly became a problem with the continued expansion of the O Neill sphere of influence. Stanley was clearly incompetent. Complaints against him began to reach England and early in 1391 the

king ordered an inquiry into the conduct of his government. The lieutenant's retinue was found to be deficient
in numbers during a muster at Naas in May and apparently
other charges against him were sustained, for on 11
September 1391 he was removed from office.

The situation continued to deteriorate. Early in 1392 the
citizens of Dublin wrote to the king, urging him earnestly
to take the government of Ireland in hand. The king's reply
was an announcement at the end of April that he would
appoint the duke of Gloucester as lieutenant of Ireland. A
major expedition was contemplated. The duke was to
serve for five years, receiving 34,000 marks for the first
three. His indenture also specified that he was to have all
the revenues of Ireland. The most interesting provision,
however, was that after three years the government of
Ireland should not only be self-supporting, but should
provide a surplus which would enable the duke to pay
annually a sum of money (to be fixed by negotiation) into
the English exchequer. During May shipping was ordered
to be collected at Bristol and the duke was soon busy
recruiting a large army. Well over £1,000 was paid out as
an advance to 52 knights and squires who were to provide
men at arms and archers for his army, and £225 was spent
on the purchase of artillery. Altogether he received 9,500
marks before the expedition was cancelled late in July.

There seems to have been earlier plans to send Gloucester
to Ireland. Certainly he himself had sought a duchy in
Ireland in 1389 and in 1391 had been given the profits and
rents of absentee lords there. His opposition to the king was
to grow fierce again, but it was not too open in 1392 to
prevent his appointment to Ireland. Very likely Gloucester
hoped that Ireland would provide status and an outlet for
his ambition. In the light of all this, it is not easy to see why
his appointment was suddenly cancelled. Possibly Richard
II felt that it would be too dangerous to let him loose in
Ireland with a large army. Gloucester must have concurred

and it may be that at the last minute he realised that Ireland was a poor place for an ambitious man. After he visited it in 1394–5 he was scathing in what he said about the lack of opportunities there.

For whatever reason, the cancellation of Gloucester's expedition was a blow to those in Ireland who had hoped for decisive intervention from England. The appointment of the earl of March as lieutenant was no consolation, since he did not come to govern in person and Ormond was forced to take office as justiciar. This was a job for which Ormond had no relish – he wrote that he was 'not capable of undertaking the governance of the land . . . in such a state as the said land is in at present, nor do we know in any way how we can sustain it without great dishonour and the destruction of our poor and simple estate'. But for two years, while the guardians of the young Mortimer argued about the conditions of his appointment, Ormond was left to govern. Representations to the king in 1393 brought some measure of relief, when some troops were sent across to Ireland in the summer. Expeditions in Munster, against the O Byrnes in Leinster, and westwards as far as Westmeath, kept Ormond busy. Still the general situation deteriorated and the need of more help from England grew. It came in a spectacular way, when Richard II decided to come in person to Ireland and solve the Irish problem once and for all. He was able to intervene because a truce had been negotiated with France and there was peace with Scotland. There was also domestic peace and the king felt sufficiently secure to be able to leave England with an easy mind.

Richard II in Ireland

The first sign of the king's intention came on 16 June 1394, when he ordered all the Irish in England to return home immediately and announced his intention of going to Ireland. It may have been in his mind for some time. A

Westminster parliament in the spring of 1393 had ordered all absentees back to Ireland. But the ordinance of 1394 was much more sweeping in its effect, since it included not only holders of land and benefices, but the craftsmen, artisans and labourers who seem to have been emigrating to England in large numbers. To judge by the number of exemptions issued during the weeks following 16 June, the ordinance was vigorously enforced by the royal officials. The purpose of the legislation, then, was not only the familiar one of getting absentees to defend their lands; it was also intended to restore a working population to areas which, presumably, had suffered losses because of the Gaelic revival. As we shall see, the king soon had radical plans for turning Leinster into a great land of peace and it was possibly here that the returning workers were to settle.

Once the decision was taken to come to Ireland, no time was lost in making the most comprehensive preparations for what would be the largest expedition ever to come to Ireland in the middle ages. The army was not only to be large – the chronicler Froissart wrote that 'it is not in memory that ever any king of England made such apparel and provision for any journey to make war against the Irishmen, nor such a number of men at arms nor archers' – but it was to be organised and financed by the king's household, so that it was very much under the personal control of the king. It was this which gave rise to the belief that Richard's autocracy was now being provided with an army and that Ireland was to be the testing ground of his military strength. This is not very likely. There were urgent reasons for military intervention in Ireland, as we have seen, and for long there had been a demand there for the presence of the king. It was natural for the king to employ troops as he could most easily find them. He had built up a large body-guard of Cheshire archers in addition to the usual household troops customarily retained by the king. Like so many of the magnates, he had also organised a large number of

O Cahan

O DONNELL   O NEILL

●Sligo   O Hanlon   Magennis
O Connor   O Ruairc   Mac Mahon
                              ●Dundalk
                   O Reilly

Lower MacWilliam Burke   O Farrel   ●Drogheda
              O Conor
              Don   O Melaghlin   ●Trim
O Kelly   O Connor
                     Faly   ●Dublin
●Galway
              O Kennedy   KILDARES
Clanrickard
Burke   O More   O Toole

O Brien   O Byrne

         ●Limerick   BUTLERS MAC MURROUGH
                          ●Kilkenny
Fitz Gerald

Fitz Gerald DESMOND   Wexford
                     Waterford● ●
         MAC CARTHY   Power

              Cork●

Ireland in 1394

III

retainers wearing his livery (the white hart) and accepting his wages. These were liable to be called up for service at any time and they now provided him with the bulk of the archers he intended to bring to Ireland. In July all 'yeomen and archers of the Crown of whatsoever condition, being at the king's wages and fees' were ordered to 'draw with all speed to the king's presence . . . ready every man according to his estate and means and arrayed to sail with the king to Ireland'. These would form the nucleus of an army, controlled by the king and directed through the household. But magnates and their retinues were also invited to join this army for pay, especially those who were absentee lords of great estates in Ireland (such as the earl of March, who was lord of Ulster, Connacht and Trim, and the earl of Nottingham, lord of Carlow).

The size of the army which the king brought to Ireland is difficult to establish at present. The surviving records indicate that something like 5,000 men at arms and archers were in the king's pay in Ireland from October 1394 onwards. But there were also Cheshire archers and others retained by the king on a permanent basis, and these may have brought numbers over 6,000. Further augmented in Ireland, this royal army was vastly greater than anything which had opposed the Gaelic revival before. The king's purpose was obviously conquest. He made adequate arrangements for the provision of arms and artillery for the expedition. Before the summer was out, a household clerk and a valet were sent ahead to Ireland with a quantity of arms from the privy wardrobe (the department which in England looked after arms, armour and artillery for the royal army), to be stored in Dublin castle until the king should need them. Then later, with the king, came the privy wardrobe itself, with much of the arms which were normally stored in the Tower of London.

Commissariat arrangements, too, were taken in hand during the summer. Household officials were sent to

Ireland early in July to 'find quarters for the entertainment of the king and the magnates coming with him in his army to Ireland, and to provide the necessary victuals therefor, at the king's charges, with power to imprison contrariants'. The sheriffs of most English counties were required to provide quantities of food for the army, presumably to feed the different contingents as they passed on their way to Milfordhaven (the port of embarkation) from all parts of England. In August household officials were ordered to arrest in England 'as many fishermen with their vessels, boats, nets, instruments and other engines as will suffice for catching fish at sea for the use of the household during the present expedition to Ireland' – a sad commentary on the state of the Irish fishing industry. The household officials (two knights) who came to Ireland to make adequate commissariat arrangements were accompanied by a small force of men – 42 men at arms, 190 mounted archers, 9 foot archers and 52 household grooms. The king must have anticipated trouble during the purveyance and was providing his purveyors with powerful military escorts. Purveyors in Ireland had bitter experience of violent opposition in the past and English experience, too, had shown the need for protection. In the event, while the purveyance in Ireland went forward, it did not produce supplies on the scale required. In September, therefore, en route to Milfordhaven, the king had to order supplies from the English counties – an order which was repeated when supplies ran short early in 1395.

Richard and his army eventually landed at Waterford on 2 October. But he did not take the field for nearly another three weeks. Naturally arrangements had to be made before a campaign could be mounted and this would account for the delay. But it is likely that the king also took counsel with his advisors and listened to Anglo-Irish advice on how best to cope with the problem. Before leaving England he had written to the duke of Burgundy that he was coming to Ireland for 'the punishment and correction of our rebels there and to establish good government and just rule over our faithful lieges'. We know from later correspondence that the English council had advised him to use 'harsh measures' in dealing with the rebels and it seems evident that the exceptionally large army he brought with him was designed to punish the chronic rebels. Leinster, of course, was the first target. The king showed great skill in his solution of the military problem. It was probably on the advice of the Anglo-Irish that he employed the traditional Irish system of warding, though the scale was greater than had been seen in Ireland before. A letter from an Englishman, who was with the king in Leinster, describes how 'our redoubted lord and king did set certain wards (*gardes*) very cunningly, as it seems to me, your poor subject, round about the Irish enemies'. He tells how the earl of Rutland was in one, with men at arms and archers, and the Marshal in another, and so on. The heavy cavalry were deployed in the open country around the wards and in sudden raids into the country of Mac Murrough. The same letter describes how the Marshal had 'several fine encounters with them, in one of which he slew many of the people of the said Mac Murrough' and how he burned nine villages, capturing 8,000 of his cattle in the process. 'And on another raid he broke in upon him and if he had not been foreseen he would have found the said Mac Murrough and his wife in their beds. But they, being told of the affray, escaped with great difficulty and at such short warning that they were very nearly taken'. They fled in such a hurry that she left behind a chest 'in which were certain articles of feminine use, but of no great value'. A much more serious loss was the seal which Mac Murrough left behind him.

The Leinster solution

These harassing raids, in which villages were burned, people killed and cattle preyed, were so effective that within ten days of the English army leaving Waterford, Mac Murrough and his leading sub-chieftains (O Byrne, O Toole and O Nolan) made their submissions and the campaign was over. Savage and swift, supported by the great wards, this brief campaign had given the king possession of Leinster. The king wrote to the English chancellor, giving him the good news: 'It seems to us that all the land of Leinster is conquered and apparently truly at peace'. Later, in January 1395, in another letter to the chancellor the king gave him the startling news that 'all our rebels of our land of Leinster have promised shortly to quit this land of Leinster, which of all others in Ireland is ever the most famous, fair and fertile, so that the same land will be, as we think, in a short time assured of peace and quiet'.

That the king expected Mac Murrough and the others to move out of Leinster was the result of a momentous agreement reached with Mac Murrough, after much deliberation, on 7 January 1395. After swearing fealty and promising the return of 'all lands, tenements, castles, fortresses, woods, and pastures with all their appurtenances' which he and his allies had occupied, Mac Murrough swore 'that by the first Sunday of Lent next he will leave the whole country of Leinster to the true obedience, use and disposition of the king'. It was also agreed that 'all the armed men, warriors, or fighting men of the following, household, or nation of the said Art shall quit the whole land of Leinster aforesaid and shall go with him and shall have fitting wages from the king, for the time being, to go and conquer other parts occupied by rebels of the said lord king, and that Art and all his men aforesaid shall have all lands which they may thus acquire and hold them of the lord king'. Similar agreements were made on the same day with O Byrne, O More, O Nolan and all the leading lords of Leinster, who promised to 'quit that country' with all their warriors. The king promised to 'maintain these captains at the expense of his household at good and fitting wages . . . for the term of their lives' and also promised to confirm them in possession of any lands they might conquer.

The king was attempting to kill two birds with one stone by means of these elaborate agreements. In the first place he would pacify Leinster; and at the same time by retaining the Gaelic lords through his household he would not only build up a body of armed retainers in Ireland which might be useful to him in some future emergency, but he was finding a means of suppressing rebels in other parts of the country. In an English context, this made sense. In an Irish context, however, there was no hope of success.

Leinster, as we have seen, had been a chronic problem since the late thirteenth century. From his own lands in north Wexford, Wicklow and Carlow, and in alliance with other lords such as O Connor of Offaly, O More of Leix, or O Byrne of Wicklow, the king of Leinster threatened the settlement in Wexford, Kilkenny, Carlow and Kildare. The annexation of the barony of Idrone by Mac Murrough was a frightening development. Strategically placed on the Barrow, it gave him such control over the main lines of communication that it made it impossible for any government to tolerate his claim (through his wife) to the barony of Norragh further north. A simple conjunction with O More of Leix was sufficient to strangle the main routes linking Dublin with south Leinster and Munster. No wonder that Art Mac Murrough and his Leinster allies seemed to Richard II the greatest danger to the security of Ireland. Raiding was regular (despite the payment of black rents or their equivalents). All attempts to deal with the problem had been futile. Only Richard II had the imagination to contemplate a real solution – expulsion of the great lords and their fighting men from Leinster and a large-scale English resettlement.

With this in mind, he revived the lordship of Carlow for the earl of Nottingham, and it was he who therefore received the submission of Mac Murrough and the other

Gaelic lords. He also made new grants of land. For example, a huge slice of territory between 'the Slaney on the south part and the Blackwater at Arklow on the north, and from the sea on the east to the borders of Kildare and Carlow on the west, except the lands and tenements which are of the earl of Ormond' was granted to John de Beaumont. Janico Dartas was given extensive lands south of Dublin which, as he said himself in a letter to the treasurer of England, if they 'were in the parts of London, would be worth by the year 50,000 marks'. William Lescrope, too, was given lands in O Byrne's country. That these grants quickly began to take effect is clear from a letter written on 18 January by Gerald O Byrne. He reminded the king that when he had surrendered all his lands and possessions the king had given the duke of Gloucester and Lescrope some of those lands, but that all the rest had been returned to O Byrne. Now, however, the earl of Ormond is claiming 'divers lands and tenements by ancient right within the said country, about which right I know nothing'.

The success of Richard's plan depended on the Gaelic lords vacating Leinster, being forced to if necessary, and on the Anglo-Irish and English magnates making good their claims and resettling their lordships. On both counts it failed. It proved impossible to dislodge the Gaelic lords when they renegued on their promises, and the new grantees soon returned to England (Nottingham straight away, Rutland soon after, and Lescrope by 1397), to swell the number of absentee Irish lords. By the time the king returned to England on 15 May 1395, his Leinster plans had begun to collapse and before long the Gaelic lords there were just as great a menace as they ever had been.

The Gaelic submissions

Meanwhile, the early success of King Richard in Leinster had produced a strong reaction elsewhere in Gaelic Ireland. Froissart in his chronicle put the question: 'How did those four kings (Mac Murrough, O Neill, O Connor and O Brien) of Ireland come so soon to the king's obeissance?' And he answered it: 'It is seen nowadays that earthly princes get little except by power and strength. The great power that the king had over with him and tarried there in their country nine months, and every man well paid, abashed them . . . But when the Irishmen saw the great number of men at war that King Richard had in Ireland this last journey, the Irishmen advised themselves and came into obeissance'. This is an exaggeration, since there was fighting outside Leinster before many Gaelic lords submitted. There was also considerable diplomatic activity, especially in the north. Nevertheless, the mere presence of the king and his great army, coupled with his swift military success in Leinster, was a powerful force in favour of submission.

By now, too, it seems that the king had changed his mind about how best to deal with the Gaelic lords. We have seen that the English council, in backing the expedition, had counselled him to use force, which Richard had successfully done in Leinster. But on 1 February 1395 Richard wrote a very remarkable letter to the regent and council in England. He divided the people of Ireland into three groups: 'the wild Irish, our enemies, the Irish rebels, and the obedient English'. It is not entirely clear which people comprised each of these groups; but it is now generally accepted that the 'wild Irish' were those who had never made formal submission to the king (such as O Donnell of the north) and the 'rebel Irish' were the Gaelic lords who had submitted in the past (such as O Neill and O Brien) and were now in rebellion. If this is true, then the king went on to make a noteworthy confession: 'the said Irish rebels are rebels only because of grievances and wrongs done to them on one side and lack of remedy on the other. If they are not wisely trusted and put in good hope of grace they will probably join our enemies'. Richard now made it his business to see that they were 'put in good hope of grace'. A letter from Niall Óg O Neill to the king refers to 'your majesty's letters stating that part cause of your coming to Ireland was that you would do justice to every man'. Other letters from Gaelic lords show the same expectations of justice. Malachy O Kelly, captain of his nation, complains that he has 'suffered infinite losses and wrongs, man-slaughter, ruin and plunderings, nor have I up to now received any amends from your offices, but am expecting recompense and grace from your Highness'. Maurice O Connor of Offaly admitted that he had formerly trans-gressed, 'but mainly because I found none to do justice between the English and me' and Niall Mór O Neill asked Richard to be 'shield and helmet of justice to me between my lord the earl of Ulster and me'.

There was considerable diplomatic activity, especially through the mediation of the archbishops, designed to produce peaceful submission. But it is clear that there was a considerable body of opinion opposed to this. O Neill warned that 'I cannot trust my own people since they see me turning away from them to your Majesty'. He had, in fact, deliberated with 'all the great men among the Irish of Ulster' and during the debate there were present 'envoys from O Brien, O Connor, Mac Carthy and many others of the southern Irish, urging us strongly not to go to the king'. In the end, however, diplomacy won and a massive series of submissions was made, involving the whole of Gaelic Ireland.

The terms of these submissions naturally varied from one individual to the next, but they generally involved fealty, with homage in a number of cases, the restoration of occupied lands, and the acceptance of the rights of mesne lords. The king's aim was to restore a framework of legal relationships between the Anglo-Irish magnates, the Gaelic lords and himself. In this way the lordship of Ireland would be reestablished in some real sense. He clearly regarded

Niall Óg O Neill (whom he called 'the great O Neill') as the most important of the Gaelic lords, which indeed he was. By January 1395 O Neill was ready to submit, but there was disagreement with Roger Mortimer, the young earl of March and Ulster, over the rights which he claimed over O Neill. The king promised to resolve the problem and on this basis both Niall Óg and his father Niall Mór eventually made submission and promised to Mortimer those services which the O Neills had traditionally given to the earls of Ulster.

But despite repeated requests, the king never resolved the outstanding problems between Mortimer and the O Neills, whether by design or neglect is not clear. In one letter (written sometime after 25 March, when O Neill, O Connor, Mac Murrough and O Brien had been knighted by the king at Dublin) O Neill looked for a remedy from the king 'against the dangers which apparently threaten me. For it is openly foretold that after your departure my lord the earl of Ulster will wage bitter war against me and if I make no resistance he will crush me without pity, so it is believed'. The prediction was to be only too true. Young and inexperienced as he was, Mortimer was the king's choice as governor of Ireland when he left in May. It was he, therefore, who was left to supervise the final completion of the settlement made by the king. Needless to say he used the opportunity to enforce his claims against O Neill, invading his lands when he encountered fierce opposition.

The collapse of Richard's settlement

Others had similarly been pushing claims against the Gaelic lords, most notably the earl of Ormond (who had acted as justiciar while the king was in Ireland). These, naturally, were fiercely resisted and before long there was widespread war again. When a message from the Westminster parliament on 13 February urged the king to return home, 'once your land of Ireland has been put in good and wise governance against your absence', it congratulated him that he had 'done well, honourably and sufficiently'. It is true that on paper much had been achieved. But the cost had been enormous and a permanent settlement would have required the presence of the king and his great army for a much longer period of time than he could afford. The February message had given another condition necessary for success: 'the deputies left in your absence for the governance of that your land must do their utmost diligently to treat your people there in good and rightful ways of justice, as we truly hope they will do'. Here, too, the king fell down, for he made no adequate arrangements before he left Ireland. The course of English politics soon even made him suspicious of Mortimer, whose uncle had been impeached in England, even though he was with his nephew in Ireland. His arrest was ordered and then in October 1397 the king announced that he intended going shortly to Ireland. Nothing came of this and eventually on 26 July the king appointed the duke of Surrey as lieutenant in place of Mortimer. There had been much bargaining before this appointment was accepted by Surrey, who insisted that he should have a man and wife from each parish, or two parishes, in England sent at the king's cost to Ireland to inhabit the march areas.

By now Mortimer had been killed in a skirmish near Carlow. He had antagonised the Gaelic lords and rebellion was widespread in Leinster and Ulster. The king's presence was urgently required if the 1395 settlement was to be salvaged. But events in England made it impossible for him to leave, until the death of John of Gaunt early in 1399 removed the main threat to the king's security in England. Even before that, preparations for an expedition were begun. In January £7,000 was transferred to the king's household for the expedition and another £6,000 not long afterwards. Still the king was not sure that it was safe to leave England and he delayed until May. He took the precaution of bringing with him as hostages the sons of his leading enemies, most notably the son of Bolingbroke (the future Henry V). So it was not until 1 June 1399 that he landed at Waterford for the second time.

The second expedition

All the evidence suggests that Richard's army on this occasion was smaller than that which came with him in 1394. But it seems to have been well equipped. As before, the privy wardrobe came with the king to Ireland and we have details of some of the stores which were left behind in Dublin castle after the king returned to England – 141 coats of mail, a huge number of bows and sheaves of arrows, a barrel full of bowstrings, 353 lances without heads, one small coffer containing 356 lance heads, 16 single canons, 16 other canons, 6 barrels full of 'stones for canons', all the paraphernalia for loading and firing canons (including 'fire pans') and one small barrel of 'gun powder'. Even though there was a shortage of money, the king was accompanied with much more pomp than in 1394. He brought a large number of ministers with him, and his embroiderer (from whom, it was said, he could not bear to be separated).

From Waterford he moved on to Kilkenny. In a letter to his uncle, the regent of England, after describing how he had a crossing 'by divine grace so favourable that no one can remember so benign a passage', the king reported the good news that Surrey had made a great attack on Mac Murrough and his allies, killing 157 'armed men and kerns'. This gave him good heart. 'We have', he wrote, 'had a very good beginning, trusting in the Almighty that He will lead us, and that shortly, to a good conclusion of our undertaking'. His hopes were rudely dashed however. He rashly penetrated into Mac Murrough's country, the army presenting the Irish with an easy target as stragglers and foraging parties were picked off. Supplies were low. A contemporary writer, Creton, describes how when the starving army finally reached the coast and three ships arrived from Dublin with food, even the knights plunged into the sea to squabble over the supplies. Mac Murrough offered to negotiate and a famous meeting took place between himself and Gloucester. Creton describes it. 'I saw Mac Murrough and a body of Irish more than I can remember descend the mountain. He rode a horse without saddle, which was so fine and good that it had cost him, they said, four hundred cows. In coming down it galloped so hard that I for certain never saw hare, deer or sheep run with such speed. In his right hand he carried a great long lance, which he cast with much skill. He was a fine, large man, wonderfully active. To look at he seemed very stern and savage and an able man'. The discussion ended in disagreement. Richard pressed on to Dublin, to prepare for a new campaign against Mac Murrough. At some stage he received word of the invasion of England by Bolingbroke, though we cannot be sure when. At any rate, he marched from Dublin to Waterford, seemingly not bothering with Mac Murrough on the way. From Waterford he sailed home, though not in time to save his throne. He left the Leinster problem unresolved behind him.

It is easy to see why he failed. Both in 1395 and 1399 time was against him. On the first occasion he had deployed his resources with remarkable success and had begun to tackle the Leinster problem in the only logical way. He may have been less than honest in his dealing with Gaelic Ireland, especially O Neill, though one must appreciate the pressures on him to safeguard the interests of the magnates. But he had neither the resources, nor one suspects the continued interest, to persist in Ireland until the problem was solved. Once he left, the situation reverted to what it had been before he intervened. Other than rebellion the great Gaelic lords had no defence against the claims of Mortimer and others like him. It is to Richard's credit that he came a second time (and lost his throne as a result, though that might have happened in any case). But the second campaign seems to have been ill-conceived from the beginning and was doomed to failure.

So two royal expeditions and a huge outlay of money by the English exchequer had done nothing to solve the problem of Ireland. This was made clear in the 1399 message from the Irish council, which paints a picture even blacker than usual. It was almost as if Richard had never come to Ireland at all. His intervention was to be the last large-scale one for a hundred years. From now on Ireland was to be left more to her own devices, with the great magnates there gaining an ascendancy in the governance of the lordship which they gradually came to regard as their right.

5 Anglo-Irish Separatism

The Financial Problem

The Irish council lost no time in establishing contact with the new government in England. No sooner had it word that Richard was a prisoner, than a long message was sent to England, painting a most dismal picture of the state of the lordship. Mac Murrough was still at open war, now allied with Desmond; O'Neill, too, was on the march. The military situation could not have been more serious. The English army had been disbanded and there was no money to raise a new army in Ireland. Then followed a terrible admission of the colony's incapacity to fend for itself: 'the Irish enemies are strong and arrogant and of great power, and there is neither rule nor power to resist them, for the English marchers are not able, nor are they willing to ride against them without stronger paramount power'. Worse, if anything, were the rebel English who were the allies of the Irish, oppressing the poor liege people. At the end of the message, special emphasis was laid on the critical state of exchequer revenues and the incompetence of exchequer officials.

The emphasis laid on finance is important, for it indicates straight away what was to be the great weakness in Lancastrian relations with Ireland. The fourteenth century had shown that only by means of financial subsidies and military aid could the English position in Ireland be maintained. The local Anglo-Irish magnates gave little thought to the financial problem, except when the tax collectors came around; they were too concerned with the problems of survival or advancement in the troubled conditions of a society in the process of change (just as their equivalents elsewhere in the collapsing world of feudalism looked to their own interests first). But hard-pressed Dublin governments, faced with the problems of the Gaelic revival and the never-ending difficulties of maintaining the rule of law, realised only too well their dependence on support from England. Successive English governments were well aware of this, and financial estimates drawn up by the council regularly made provision for 'the war in Ireland', 'the defence of Ireland', or the requirements of military chief governors on their way across the Irish sea. It was the Lancastrians who defaulted and thereby created a situation of great political danger in Ireland.

For various reasons, the Lancastrian governments were chronically short of money. They were never able to call on sufficient funds to meet all their military commitments. So they had to fall back on complicated credit operations. They regularly anticipated revenues in the form of assignments whereby their servants received tallies, not cash, which were supposedly cashable at the source of revenue on which they were drawn. At times of chronic financial crises, too many of such tallies were issued and proved to be uncashable. They had, therefore, to be exchanged for new ones, which sometimes proved to be uncashable as well. It might take years for a man to recover all that was owing to him, and some unfortunates never caught up.

Bad tallies for Ireland

It is a significant fact that the first lieutenant of Ireland appointed by the new Lancastrian government, John Stanley, received the first £1,000 of his salary in tallies and not in cash. The pattern was set for the future: rarely were the governors of Ireland to receive cash. But worse, Stanley got tallies which proved to be uncashable (as late as 1 June

1403, three worth £1,500 were replaced), so that by June 1401 he was reduced to the ignominious position where the king had to order a respite for his debts in Ireland, as he could not pay them. This, too, was to be part of the pattern for the future: not only was payment normally by means of tallies, but all too often they were uncashable.

Nowhere is this better illustrated than in the case of the king's son, Thomas of Lancaster, sent to govern Ireland late in 1401. He was granted 12,000 marks a year, but almost immediately he was in financial difficulties. In August 1402 the king was reduced to relying on the good will of a London mercer, who went bond for him for £150 to two merchants of Lucca, which went to Thomas in Ireland; and two other Londoners, one a mercer and the other a skinner, also lent money for the same purpose. But in that same month a message from Ireland informed the king of the financial embarrassment of his son, 'so destitute of money that he has not a penny in the world, nor can he borrow a penny, for all his jewels and plate, beyond what he must keep of necessity, are put and remain in pledge'. His soldiers had deserted for want of pay, and even the members of his own household were beginning to leave. By June 1403, he was over £9,000 in arrears and four years later the figure had climbed to over £20,000. Years afterwards he was still receiving bad tallies for these old debts.

If the king could treat his own son in this way, other chief governors could hardly expect to fare better. Nor did they. John Talbot, earl of Shrewsbury, for all his great influence at court and the prestige of his name, could never catch up on what was owing to him for service in Ireland. In February 1434, the English council agreed to pay him £1,000 for his service in France and Ireland, though he was owed far more: this was an agreed settlement, 'the said lord promising to make no further demand'. Sir Thomas Stanley, who was appointed lieutenant in 1431, was owed 5,000 marks by the beginning of 1434. Lord

Welles, who had been appointed lieutenant in February 1438, was in office for just three years. Yet in April 1442, he was still owed 3,000 marks. The White earl of Ormond was luckier than most, since he was able to pass on £300 of bad tallies to John Talbot in 1445 as part of the dowry he gave his daughter when she married Talbot's son.

Such examples could be multiplied. No chief governor escaped. Apart from the oppressions which resulted from lack of adequate revenues in Ireland – for example, soldiers regularly had to be billeted on the people and many of them, deserting for want of pay, became an even greater burden on the community – much valuable time had to be wasted by governors in importuning the English government for arrears in stipend. But hard-pressed Lancastrian governments had little money to spare for Ireland and the records of council meetings make it quite clear that Irish needs were very far down on any list of financial priorities. When the English council on 5 May 1421 discussed the disposal of revenues for the year, only 2,500 marks (or £1,666.13.4) out of nearly £56,000 were set aside 'for the guarding of the land in Ireland'.

With their financial position so bad, these governments had to allocate their revenues carefully and often had to decide between conflicting claims. Here, too, Ireland came off badly. Calais, for example, normally had to come first. In the summer of 1403, when the king's son was in danger in Ireland because of gross default in the payment of his stipend, an order was made that he was to have new assignments on the wool custom of Hull, 'notwithstanding any assignments made on the same, except grants and annuities made by the king before this and what is assigned for the safe custody of the town of Calais and the marches there'. A year later, when a complicated set of assignments on different ports was made so as to pay him arrears, assignments for Calais were again given priority, as they were in April and then in July 1405. In March 1437, the treasurer in

England, Lord Hungerford, made the position in Ireland crystal clear: he petitioned the council that 'a memorandum should be made that notwithstanding any warrant which had previously been issued to him for the payment of Sir Thomas Stanley, lieutenant of Ireland, preference should be given to other payments touching the security of the king's person and the affairs of France'. In February 1434 he had been even more direct, when he told the council that 'he does not dare pay or assign the said wages' because of the pressing need of money elsewhere.

The revenues of Ireland

There was a long queue, then, for back pay at the English exchequer and more often than not the governors of Ireland were back near the end of the line. Some of them undoubtedly suffered serious personal losses (though we may be sure that they recouped themselves in other ways while in Ireland); but usually the real losers were the soldiers in pay, the people who supplied the necessary provisions for the governors, their households and retinues, and the many who had a financial claim, for one reason or another, on the government. There was no hope that the Irish revenues would help to make up the deficit to any appreciable extent, despite the fact that governors were now regularly granted the revenues of Ireland without being accountable for them. Some governors were lucky. Stephen Lescrope received £256.13.4 from Irish revenues in 1404 and John Talbot just over £1,000 in 1414. But most got little if anything. Thomas Stanley, for example, was supposed to be paid 1,000 marks in each of the four exchequer terms to make up his stipend of 4,000 marks. In Easter term 1417, he only received £37.3.4; in the two terms of St John and Michaelmas only 50½ marks; the next two terms he got nothing at all; and the next Michaelmas term only four marks. Indeed Stanley had earlier complained that despite the terms of his indenture, he received nothing from the issues of Ireland, because 'after grants, charges and payments', nothing was left in the exchequer.

Irish finances during this period are obscure and it is not possible, from the fragmentary records which survive, to give any kind of detailed picture of the income and expenditures of Irish governments. But it is easy enough to show that income was low, usually around £1,000 per annum. There was not enough money to regularly meet annual expenses and the stipends of royal officials, even the treasurer himself, were normally in arrears. In 1441, Giles Thorndon, the treasurer, told the English council that 'the charges of the justiciar of Ireland and his officials this year exceed the revenues by £1,456'. This may have been an unusually high adverse balance; but it is a fair indication of a normal situation, when no chief governor could count on being able to avail of a surplus revenue in Ireland.

The Pale

With limited financial resources, it was only to be expected that the government would be seriously restricted in its military operations. It tended, therefore, to fall back on defensive measures in the main, concentrating its efforts on securing the frontiers of the land of peace. More and more this area became closely identified with the English parts of counties Dublin, Meath, Kildare and Louth. Indeed there is evidence that before the middle of the fifteenth century an area clearly identified as a Pale had developed, though its precise limitations are not known.

The Pale emerged from the political circumstances of fifteenth-century Ireland. The real problem for any government was the lack of any one Gaelic dynasty, possessing wide authority, with whom the chief governor could treat. Relations had to be secured and maintained with a large number of autonomous lords, none of whom followed any fixed principle other than self-interest. To make matters worse, few of these dynasts enjoyed permanent

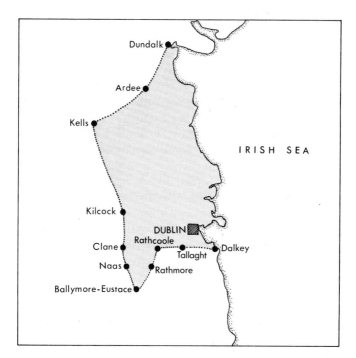

The Pale in 1515

tenure of lordship, so that the government might find a carefully negotiated settlement destroyed by the sudden winds of change which followed internecine strife. To complicate matters even more, the government found itself unable to exercise effective control over its own local communities, which again were motivated by self-interest and dealt with Irish enemies as expedience and convenience dictated. The situation, in short, was impossible for established centralised forms of government. Stability was restored to Ireland when this fact was recognised, tacitly at least, and an equilibrium created on the basis of the network of lordships which covered Ireland. The lords, Gaelic and Anglo-Irish, formed their own alliances and ententes; the government confined itself mainly to its immediate sphere of influence in the eastern part of the island. This produced the idea of a Pale, possibly inspired by the familiar Pale of Calais.

In 1404 an important meeting of council was held in Dublin, where a decision was taken to recover Ulster. The reason for this new aggressive policy is very revealing: the council was told that otherwise the Irish enemies would have 'full entry without impediment into the counties of Louth and Meath to destroy and devastate'. This clearly shows the defensive mentality which lay behind the emergence of a Pale. In time sections of the new frontier were fortified with castles and fortalices. Important bridges were guarded and other parts were entrenched. Watchmen along the frontier were paid to keep watch and light warning beacons, a special tax (called, appropriately, *smokesilver*) being levied to pay their wages. The area covered varied from time to time. Despite the precise definitions of the extent of the Pale given in the sixteenth century, there is no doubt that for much of the fifteenth it was a concept which was given only the vaguest territorial expression. Furthermore, while the inhabitants naturally feared the loss of life which raids by the Irish enemies or English rebels naturally provoked, it was loss of stock which was their primary concern. Taking preys of cattle was now a principal feature of Irish warfare, amongst the Anglo-Irish no less than in Gaelic Ireland. An extraordinary act of the 1456 parliament, which provided that the church of St George in Dublin was to receive one out of every 40 cows preyed by the gentlemen of Kildare and the other three counties, is a vivid reminder of how much of warfare was in fact devoted to preying.

When, therefore, the inhabitants of the Pale built their trenches it was not so much to keep the Irish out as to prevent them from taking cattle out. An act of parliament in 1475 describes how a dyke had been built from Tallaght to Saggart, which was now broken in different places by Irish enemies, English rebels and 'by divers persons dwelling on the frontier of the march, whereby the aforesaid Irish enemies and English rebels have committed many and great robberies in the king's lands'. The thirty-fourth act of Poynings' parliament of 1495, 'for ditches to be made about the English Pale', shows the same preoccupation with the 'great hurts' which the Irish do by their forays 'and making of preys'.

Relations with Gaelic lords

Keeping the frontiers of the Pale safe was the essence of the military policy of most fifteenth-century governments. At first Richard II's policy of containment was continued, as governments tried to force submission from leading Gaelic lords on the perimeter of the Pale. Stephen Lescrope brought in O Connor of Offaly and O Byrne of Leinster; Thomas of Lancaster brought in Mac Mahon of Louth and O Reilly of Cavan. Early in the reign of Henry IV a great council in Dublin, composed of representatives of the four counties and including some from Carlow, decided to send an army to recover parts of Ulster and colonise them, so as to prevent the Irish and Scots enemies from having an easy entry into Meath and Louth.

Official policy, then, was to force the Gaelic lords on the frontier of the pale into submission. The form usually involved a promise to be a faithful liege of the king, a restoration of stolen property, return of prisoners, cessation of blackrent and sometimes a promise of military help. When the great English captain John Talbot came to Ireland he vigorously pursued this policy. A long report from a council meeting at Naas at the end of June 1417 gives a detailed account of how well he succeeded. He 'made many great journies and hostings upon one of the strongest Irish enemies of Leinster called O More of Leix', forcing him to submit and to join him with two 'battles' (450 men in each division) of horse and foot against Mac Mahon. O Byrne and O Reilly made similar submissions and joined the expedition against Mac Mahon. He, too, submitted and supported Talbot against O Connor of Offaly. On the borders of Ulster, O Hanlon had his lands devastated and had to sue for peace. The great Gaelic lords of Ulster, O Neill, O Neill Boy, McGuinness, O Donnell and Maguire took fright and made their peace. The report emphasised Talbot's success in securing 'the frontier of the borders of the Irish enemies of Leix'. He fortified the bridge at Athy, making the entry of enemies impossible. He finally forced Maurice O Keating of Dublin to submit: 'for himself and his nation [he] yielded himself to the same your lieutenant without any condition and with his breast against his sword's point and a cord around his neck'.

The Anglo-Irish lords

No chief governor could afford to dispense with the help of the local Anglo-Irish lords. If he were Anglo-Irish himself, like an earl of Ormond, he was in a position to use family connexions and old alliances to help preserve peace in the localities. The fourth (or 'white') earl of Ormond is an excellent example of how the powerful Anglo-Irish magnate had to involve himself intimately in the problem of maintaining peace in his own locality. Typically he worked through a network of alliances to maintain some degree of equilibrium. He was related, by marriage at least, to the Kildare Geraldines, Mac Murroughs, O Carrolls, O Reillys and the Desmond Geraldines. His influence was manifested in 1423 when his removal from office as chief governor was followed by widespread risings by the leading Gaelic lords. In a famous set of ordinances (the 'ordinances of the white earl'), which attempted to cope with the outstanding problems of his own great lordship, and notably those of defence, coyne and livery and other services which were illegal were regulated by him. It was generally recognised that illegal imposts of this kind were necessary and they were widespread throughout Anglo-Ireland. There were abuses, of course, which produced complaints such as that of the Irish parliament of 1422, which denounced the imposition of coyne ('divers sums of money each week') by the soldiers and was especially bitter about the illegal burdens imposed by the Geraldines, Burkes, Powers, 'and other great nations of the land'. The Anglo-Irish lord, of course, was able to employ a fair measure of autonomy in his lordship and this in turn made him resentful of all attempts to control him from Dublin, especially by English-born officials. Separatist tendencies had manifested themselves early in the Anglo-Irish community and there can be no doubt that these became stronger in the fifteenth century, reaching a peak in the 1460 parliament which pronounced Ireland to be 'corporate of itself'.

Feuds and factions

But it was rather the desire to control the great offices (and especially the chief governorship) and the power that went with them which was the driving force behind much of fifteenth-century Irish politics. Factions were no new addition to the Irish scene, but they now became more prominent in the struggle for power. A powerful patron and protector was essential in an age when the sword was often the most important charter a man could possess. A Gaelic poet, addressing a praise poem to a Burke in the mid-fifteenth century, expressed the situation pithily: 'The law of the Saxon kings has often been broken; the Gaill set no store by legal document; none of them obeying the king's law, each of them is an earl for himself. About Eire the principle of them all is respect for the strong man . . . a man's inheritance will get no recognition except he has strength to fight'.

Everyone had to depend on patronage, not least in the acquisition or retention of office. There was a hierarchy of privilege from the highest offices in the lordship to the lowest. When, for example, the office of clerk of the markets in Kilkenny fell vacant in 1414, Ralph Standish, the escheator, had to be bribed with a payment of 46s.4d. before the office could be filled. Early in the fourteenth century the steward of the countess of Pembroke in Waterford claimed allowances for a long series of bribes which he had to pay to various officials in Dublin – 40s. to the treasurer and 10s. to his clerks for procuring a delay in accounting at the exchequer; a carcase of beef to a justice of the bench to induce him to be lenient to an offender; 26s.8d. to two barons of the exchequer 'to have respite of the service of Dundalk and 3s. given to three ushers there'. The accounts of the priory of the Holy Trinity, Dublin, contain similar bribes – 2s. 8d. 'in cloth bought and given to the purveyors of the justiciar of Ireland that they may be more favourable to us'; 3s.4d. to a clerk of the chancellor 'to have his counsel and help for procuring a certain writ'; 5½ marks for a present to the treasurer and 5 marks for a present of wine to the chancellor. Everyone had his price – it was an accepted part of the privilege which went with office.

The holding of office, then, was something to be prized and it is no wonder that it gave rise to disputes. Here, the powerful patron, the man who controlled the greater offices, came into his own. A clash of patrons, or a clash of interests, could lead to a feud between rival factions. The greatest feud, which dominated Ireland for thirty years, involved the Ormond Butlers, the Talbots and their respective supporters. Even when the main feud was settled, in typical medieval fashion, by marriage between Talbot's son and Ormond's daughter in 1444, some of the supporters continued the quarrel. This produced one of the most colourful episodes in the whole affair, when the prior of Kilmainham, Thomas fitz Gerald, challenged the earl of Ormond to a trial by battle in London. The king not only provided suitable arms and armour for the prior, but also hired an expert to coach him in the finer points of duelling. Ormond, however, failed to appear and the prior won by default.

Behind the great quarrel there certainly lay a deep animosity between the two principals, Ormond and Talbot. From the time he was given livery of his lands in 1412, Ormond was the dominant figure among the Anglo-Irish. His expectation was that he would control the government. The arrival as chief governor of Talbot, an absentee lord with interests in Westmeath and later Wexford and a clear determination to augment these interests, was a shock. From the beginning, then, a degree of animosity existed. Talbot certainly wasted little time before attacking the earl and in July 1417 had taken his estates into the king's hands. He also lost no time in pushing his own and his family's interests and in building up a body of support which he would use to further undermine Butler ascendancy. In this way the quarrel escalated, involving more people and making ever more important control of the government and the rights of patronage that went with it. On that level the personal elements in the quarrel became less important. It was easy, too, for constitutional under-currents to cause the occasional eddy. A feature of the whole affair was the continuous mud slinging through charges and counter charges brought before the English council. A stream of messages reached the king. Control of such messages, attacking Irish governments, became imperative and this involved a greater emphasis on the importance of the Irish parliament and a closer assertion of its authority. That this might be designed to serve faction interests did not prevent the growth of parliamentary independence, which was to be given complete expression in the 1460 declaration that Ireland was a corporation, bound only by its own laws and customs. At one stage, too, Magna Carta was invoked as a guarantee of individual right and in 1418 Talbot uncovered a conspiracy when he arrested the earl of Kildare, Sir John Bellew and Sir Christopher Preston. The latter was found to be in possession of what the govern-ment considered to be incriminating documents, a copy of the English coronation oath and a famous tract on the nature of parliament. The tract has since occasioned much dispute among historians; but there can be no doubt that Talbot considered it to be subversive, a threat in some way to himself, giving some kind of constitutional basis to the opposition.

But the struggle was mainly one for power. Each side had its ups and downs, largely depending on who had the ear of the English government. On only one occasion did the factions oppose each other in the open, in 1429. When shots were fired, they took the form of accusation and counter-accusation of misgovernment and oppression, peculation and even treason before the English council, the seizure of lands and property, promotion to or dismissal from office, and outright refusal to cooperate when the opposition was in control. In 1417 the chancellor refused to seal a message of complaint from the Dublin parliament to the king. Much later, in 1442, another chancellor absconded with the great seal, making government virtually impossible for a time.

Harmful effects of factions

The persistence of quarrels involving struggles for control of the government naturally had a detrimental effect on the maintenance of law and order in Ireland, and was later held to be mainly responsible for the steady decline of English control. Writing an official report on the state of Ireland in 1427, Archbishop Swayne of Armagh painted a most dismal picture: 'in good faith the English ground that is obeying to the king's law in this land, as I suppose, is not so much of quantity as is one shire of England'. The 'husband people' had left in large numbers, because of bad government and the constant wars. His considered opinion was that the struggle between the factions grouped around Ormond and Talbot had so divided Ireland ('so all this land is severed') that 'gentlemen and commons love not other and this debate betwyx these two lords is cause of the great harms that be done in the country'.

Swayne probably exaggerated the effect of the quarrel, though it does seem that each time there was an outburst of rivalry the military situation deteriorated. Some years later the treasurer, Giles Thorndon, blamed the quarrel for much of the deterioration which had taken place in the quality of government. Many of the complaints and reports sent to England, when stripped of their polemic, reveal the failure of successive governments to provide protection which local communities craved. It is true, as we have seen, that the central government was no longer regularly concerned with outlying areas and the problems of the land of war. In the first years of the century some effort, however fitful, was made at retaining some element of control over even the more outlying parts. But this was soon found to be impossible to maintain. The message which the Irish council sent to England with the lieutenant, Sir Thomas

Stanley, in 1435 made it clear that large areas had more or less been abandoned by the Dublin government. The criterion of abandonment was the failure of chief governors to visit these parts, except for fleeting 'hostings', and the fact that neither parliaments nor courts of justice were any longer held outside the vicinity of a small area near Dublin. The complaints from towns such as Waterford, Cork, Drogheda and many smaller places echo the same feeling of abandonment and isolation, conveying a sense of beleaguerment by Irish enemies and English rebels. A petition from Waterford in 1388 described the 'arsons, homicides and thefts of the king's Irish enemies and English rebels and the invasions of other enemies of the parts adjacent' and complained of the 'capture of ships, barges and other vessels and the ransom of their men by the French and Spaniards'. In later fifteenth-century complaints the traditional enemies (the Irish and the English rebels) are regularly linked with Bretons, Spaniards and Scots.

The security problem

It is clear, then, that not only was there an alarming deterioration in the situation in Ireland, but that from early in the fifteenth century at least she presented a security problem to the shaky Lancastrian dynasty. Henry IV's insecurity at the beginning of his reign was evident. Within three months of his 'taking upon him the royal estate' (as he put it himself) part of England was in rebellion. There was danger everywhere and he was horrified to discover in mid-December 1399 that writs still ran in the name of Richard and that the great seal and other seals there still bore his name. In the same month he ordered the 1380 Statute of Absentees to be rigorously enforced and appointed John Stanley as lieutenant, with a retinue of 100 men at arms (including himself) and 300 archers. In

September 1400 the rebellion of Owen Glendower in Wales gave a new dimension to the problem of security, for the Welshman tried to involve Gaelic Ireland as well as Scotland in his challenge of the Lancastrian dynasty. Owen's appeal is interesting, because he based it on common antipathy to the Saxons and affinity of race, and he shrewdly pointed out that by keeping the forces of the king busy on his side of the Irish sea he was giving Gaelic Ireland the opportunity for successful rebellion.

His grandiose plan came to nothing; but it must have frightened Henry when the letters to Ireland and Scotland fell into his hands. Much worse, however, was the defection of Edmund Mortimer to the side of Glendower in 1402. He was the uncle of the young earl of March, who was the real heir to the throne. Here was real danger. With the Mortimers holding vast estates in Ireland and enjoying widespread support there was a danger of rebellion there. No wonder that the king decided to send his second son Thomas to Ireland as lieutenant. At all costs Ireland must be prevented from becoming a base for rebels.

In the event nothing happened. But the security problem presented by Ireland had been raised. Though the question was to lie dormant for many years, it came to the surface in a spectacular fashion in mid-century, at the height of the wars of the roses, and thereafter it became a key factor in Anglo-Irish relations. In the meantime at least one member of the English council became acutely conscious of England's security and wrote a famous tract (a *libelle* or 'little book') which he called *The Libelle of Englyshe Polycye*. It was composed in the mid-1430s, at a time when the English position in France was being seriously threatened, and in particular Calais, the seat of the staple. The author (almost certainly Adam Moleyns, clerk to the council) argued the importance of trade and therefore emphasised how much the interest of England depended on control of the sea:

> Cherish merchandise, keep the admiralty,
> That we be masters of the narrow sea.

Mastery of the sea involved Ireland and Wales, each of which was 'a buttress and a post under England', necessary for defence. In addition, Ireland was a fertile land, with good bays, rich in produce for export, enjoying a lucrative trade. But there was great potential danger there, should a king emerge who might ally himself with the Scots, French and Spaniards, the enemies of England. The fear that Ireland might become a link in a chain of enemies around England is an extraordinary anticipation of a similar, and more realistic, fear later in the century. It highlighted the security problem which Ireland might present to England.

Moleyns had a great interest in Ireland and was at one time put forward as successor to Archbishop Swayne of Armagh. Indeed, he promised to compose another *libelle*, devoted exclusively to Ireland. He was therefore an informed writer. For example, he quotes the earl of Ormond who proclaimed (in exasperation, one suspects, and with excusable exaggeration) that the expenses of one year's war in France would be sufficient to conquer Ireland. Moleyns seems to agree with him and condemns the neglect of Ireland as dangerous. What is needed there above all, considering Ireland's importance in the defence of England, is good government. But instead, he says, 'dead is governance'. The result is that enemies are in the ascendancy:

> Our money spent all to little avail,
> And our enemies so greatly do prevail.

As clerk to the council, Moleyns would be well aware of the constant stream of complaints from Ireland, highlighting bad government, the growth in power of the Irish enemies and English rebels, and prophesying that Ireland would be lost unless some immediate remedy was forthcoming.

The great lordships

The truth was, as we have seen already, that what was happening was a shift in the centre of power from Dublin to the great lordships. From the point of view of the inhabitants of the dwindling land of peace, and therefore the view of the English government, the situation in Ireland was indeed perilous and chaotic. But from an internal point of view, despite all the 'wars' and the seeming anarchy reported in contemporary sources, it is clear that a new equilibrium was being achieved which had little to do with the Dublin government. The lords, Gaelic as well as Anglo-Irish, were organising their own communities to be as self-sufficient and autonomous as possible. The rights of the lord in his own territory were being more closely defined, sometimes through the issuing of ordinances (such as the famous ones of the white earl of Ormond), sometimes by means of treaties, indentures or pacts with subservient 'clans' or 'nations' or individuals (such as the extraordinary agreements negotiated by the bishop of Cloyne in 1402–3 and preserved in the so-called *Pipe roll of Cloyne*). Rights were won or enforced through war as well. In return, the lord offered protection to his people and their leaders. This, again, might mean a hosting. But all the evidence goes to show that punitive expeditions were mainly old-fashioned cattle raids, involving little loss of life. Indeed, if we are to believe the evidence of John Talbot, writing in 1415, the making of war had by then been confined to a kind of open season, between 17 March and 29 September. This helped to maintain peace in the localities through much of the year. Another powerful agent for peace must have been marriage alliances, not just between the great families, but the lesser ones as well. About 1426 a petition to the pope to permit a marriage within the forbidden degrees of affinity between a Roger Mac Mahon of the diocese of Clogher and an Alice White contained the argument that 'therefrom probably peace will be strengthened between the English and the Irish'.

143

The growth in self-reliance among the Anglo-Irish communities, though inevitable, made them resentful of interference from England, especially through English-born chief governors. In particular the magnates resented a heavy handed governor who did not understand the local situation and who tried to apply non-Irish solutions. A strong chief governor with a vigorous military policy was often only a nuisance.

Almost from the very beginning of the English colonisation of Ireland the magnates and the communities had been left to go their own way with the minimum of interruption or direction. Self-reliance and self-sufficiency were qualities which were especially prized in the frontier conditions which prevailed in many parts of Ireland. Associated with this there naturally developed customs which were peculiar to Ireland and sometimes at variance with the common law. It was a short step from this to the claim that ancient custom established the supremacy of writs under the Irish great seal over writs out of England and to the claim of the 1441 council at Naas that all pleas could be determined in Irish courts. This could lead to a clash of authority, as happened in the 1440s when appointments under English seals were challenged by the Irish government during the final stages of the Talbot-Ormond struggle. Self-interest was the moving force in such cases. It is not easy, however, to prove that claims of this kind did not also arise from well-entrenched separatist tendencies among the Anglo-Irish. Certainly the claim that Ireland was not bound by statutes out of England, which was the final stage in the evolution of an independent Irish lordship, can hardly have been entirely motivated by self-interest. No less an authority than the famous English jurist Sir John Fortescue held that Ireland was independent in this way. He said: 'And further, the territory of Ireland is separate from the kingdom of England, for if a tenth or a fifteenth be granted here, it shall not bind the people of Ireland, and if a statute be made here, it shall not bind those in Ireland unless they approve it in their own parliament, even though the king under his great seal shall send the same statute to Ireland'. It was an Irish parliament, in 1460, which proclaimed its independence in the most solemn way possible. One of its statutes declared: 'That whereas the land of Ireland is, and at all times has been, corporate of itself by the ancient laws and customs used in the same, freed of the burden of any special law of the realm of England save only such laws as by the lords spiritual and temporal and commons of the said land had been in great council or parliament there held, admitted, accepted, affirmed and proclaimed, according to sundry ancient statutes thereof made'. It was the supreme example of Anglo-Irish separatism, and even if its validity was later challenged, the fact that such a declaration was made is memorable.

Richard of York and Ireland

The immediate purpose of this 1460 parliament was to protect Richard duke of York, who had fled to Ireland after his defeat in England. York had long since been implicated in Irish affairs. Family connexion (he was heir to the vast Mortimer lordships in Ireland) would have involved him in any event. But the course of English politics led to his appointment as lieutenant of Ireland in 1447. Contemporary opinion, reflected in a recently discovered English chronicle, was that he was manoeuvred into going to Ireland in order to get him out of the way in England. But there was a real need in Ireland for someone like York, enormously wealthy (he had an income of over £6,000 a year), experienced, and highly regarded by both Anglo-Irish and Gaelic communities. Besides, it is clear from subsequent events that York himself was anxious to build up a power base in Ireland, possibly looking to some future contingency when it might prove useful. Political ambition, too, played its part in bringing York to Ireland.

There was much hard bargaining before he agreed to accept the appointment. The first indenture of 30 July was followed by a second in September. York got exceptionally good terms. Not only was he given the revenues of Ireland without being accountable, together with the right to appoint a deputy, it was agreed that he 'shall not be held to account for the men of his retinue nor for the sums of money which he receives from our said sovereign the king for the office of lieutenancy of the said land of Ireland'. He had power to dispose of all revenues and all offices. No pardons were to be issued and no offices were to be confirmed without the assent of the lieutenant. York, in fact, was much more of a viceroy than his predecessors had been.

He was well received when he came to Ireland, Gaelic as well as Anglo-Irish lords flocking to meet him. He made the most determined effort for generations to pacify the country, procuring a wide range of submissions in Ulster, the midlands and Leinster. What is important about these is that they were made personally to York, on his own behalf and not just on behalf of the king. For example, when O Byrne came in he swore to be liegeman of the duke and his heirs. York was making the most of his opportunities in Ireland to retain people as supporters for the future. On 28 July 1450, the most powerful of the Anglo-Irish, the fourth earl of Ormond, sealed an indenture of retinue with York, binding him for life 'to do him service as well in war as in peace, as well in England when he shall happen to be there as in Ireland'. It was the same earl whom York left behind as his deputy when he returned to England a short time afterwards.

But by then his early successes had been swept away. As always happens, arrears of his stipend began to mount and lack of money made any sustained war effort impossible. By the spring of 1450 York's settlements were breaking down. Soon many of those who had submitted to him were rising. In June his own lands in Meath were being wasted – Rathmore and other villages were destroyed. In a letter to his brother-in-law at this time, York complained bitterly of the failure of the king to meet his obligations to him and expressed his fear of the disastrous consequences in Ireland. He would return to England lest he be held responsible for what might happen: 'for it shall never be chronicled nor remain in scripture, by the grace of God, that Ireland was lost through my negligence'. By the time he sailed for England in the late summer of 1450, things were as bad as ever.

The rebellion of Jack Cade in England was an embarrassment to York, not least because he claimed to be an Irish Mortimer and a relative of the duke's (an entry on an issue roll of the English exchequer describes him as 'Jack Cade of Ireland born, calling himself John Mortimer'). But York had more pressing reasons for returning home. He was heavily involved in court politics from now on and a party gradually coalesced around him. Ireland inevitably became involved especially after the new earl of Ormond, who succeeded the white earl in 1452, became one of the leaders of the opposition to York in England. His family connexions in Ireland naturally followed his lead and this inevitably strengthened Yorkist support among the Geraldines and their allies. By the time York was forced to fly for his life in the autumn of 1459, his supporters controlled the offices of government in Ireland. It is significant that he came here, sending his son and the earl of Warwick to Calais. In Ireland he was safe, protected by the government. Despite his attainder by the Coventry parliament, his lieutenancy of Ireland was confirmed by an Irish parliament. When an unfortunate messenger arrived from England carrying writs ordering the arrest of York, he was arrested, tried, found guilty of treason against the person of the duke and executed.

It was from Ireland that an invasion of England was

147

planned. York may have raised men here, cashing in on the widespread support he enjoyed. An act of the 1460 parliament gave leave to absent themselves from Ireland to all those who wished to sail with him to England. But the duke did not leave Ireland until after he had news of the defeat of the royal army at Northampton by his son and Warwick and it is unlikely, even if an army did accompany him from Ireland, that it played any significant part in the events which followed, leading to his defeat and death in December. It was the Yorkist victory at Towton in March 1461 which finally secured the crown of England for Edward, eldest son of the duke.

But within Ireland itself, where Yorkist support was widespread, there was considerable danger because of the Butler attachment to the house of Lancaster and the traditional opposition to the Geraldines (now the main buttress of Yorkist support). The acts of the 1460 parliament made it clear that there were enemies within – indeed one act suggested that a certain Richard Bermingham had gone to England to procure an invasion of Ireland and another that Gaelic chieftains had been encouraged to make war on York. Queen Margaret, wife of Henry VI, tried to stir up rebellion in Ireland, and when Sir John Butler, brother of the executed fifth earl of Ormond, landed in 1462, he received a surprising measure of support. There was rebellion not only in Kilkenny and Tipperary (which were Butler strongholds) but, more surprisingly, in Meath as well, where 'the commons of the county of Meath to the number of 5,000 made insurrection and rising', according to a message sent to Edward IV by the parliament of 1463.

Edward IV and Desmond

The same parliament issued a remarkable proclamation on behalf of the earl of Desmond, deputy of the lieutenant, emphasising the great service which he had done to the duke of York when he came to Ireland, his defeat of the Butlers, and his restoration of the land to 'rest, peace and tranquillity'. A message to the king asked him to 'have him in tenderness and special favour and him thereupon heartily thank and reward after his most wisdom and bounty'. By then Edward had already appointed Desmond as deputy and had rewarded him in other ways for his services. Given the king's character, however (he was strong-willed, determined to be his own master, the founder of the 'new monarchy' in England), he was obviously not the sort of man to remain dependent forever on the good offices of someone like Desmond. Sooner or later he was certain to apply to Ireland the methods of government which were to prove so successful in England. The first real sign of his determination to be free of Desmond was the appointment of John Tiptoft, earl of Worcester, as deputy in 1467. What followed was to show the king how independent the Anglo-Irish had become and how widespread Geraldine influence was.

Desmond, as might be expected with someone of such power and position, had plenty of enemies in Ireland. He was very unpopular in Meath, for example, where there had been such surprising support for the Butlers. The bishop of Meath, William Sherwood, emerged as the leader of the opposition in Ireland. The parliament of 1463, which had praised Desmond to the skies, also asked the king to give no attention to accusations against him, which again indicates considerable opposition. Charges were in fact laid against him in the summer of 1463 and he and Sherwood appeared before the king. Desmond cleared himself and was retained in office. But the episode showed the king that he could count on opposition to Desmond in Ireland, which made it all the easier to replace him. The fact, too, that 1466 was an unhappy year for the earl, with widespread risings following his own defeat and ignominious capture in Offaly, gave the king an excuse.

The seriousness of Edward's purpose is illustrated by the man chosen to replace Desmond. Tiptoft had been a supporter of York and on his return to England from his travels in the Holy Land and Italy (he was a scholar and noted book collector) he was not only made a member of the king's council, but appointed constable of the Tower, then constable of England, and was made a Knight of the Garter. He was also an efficient and ruthless man, earning the unhappy nickname of 'butcher of England'. He came to Ireland better prepared than any chief governor for many years, with a very large retinue of 700 archers (obviously expecting trouble) and the promise of plenty of funds from England. Parliament was summoned immediately he arrived. It met at Dublin on 11 December. During this first session, which witnessed no unusual legislation, the deputy and some others, including the earl of Kildare, founded a chantry at Dunshaughlin. The next session was switched to Drogheda, an anti-Geraldine town, and met on 4 February 1468. The very first act mounted an attack on Desmond, Kildare and Edward Plunket, attainting them of 'horrible treasons and felonies contrived and done by them' by allying with and helping the Irish. Desmond had very foolishly attended (perhaps he was ignorant of the move against him); he was arrested and executed on 15 February – 'extorciously slain and murdered by colour of the laws within Ireland . . . against all manhood, reason and good conscience', as Richard III later put it in a letter to the murdered earl's son.

Such an extreme act must have had a powerful motive behind it. The old tradition that the queen, Elizabeth Woodville, brought it about in revenge for a disparaging remark made by Desmond can be dismissed. It is unlikely, too, that Tiptoft acted independently, despite the accusation against the treasurer, Roland fitz Eustace, of having incited Desmond to rebel against the deputy and make himself king of Ireland. There may have been a plot against

Tiptoft, but he would hardly have dared to proceed so far unless he had the support of the king. It is most likely that Edward himself was responsible and that Tiptoft was his instrument. The removal of the two earls (with Ormond already out of the way) and the confiscation of their estates would enormously enhance his power in Ireland.

At any rate, either Edward or Tiptoft, or both of them, miscalculated. There was a violent reaction in Ireland to the execution. A report from the lords in parliament in June said that Gerot, brother of the murdered earl, had invaded Meath with 20,000 galloglasses and 2,000 horsemen. Other areas, too, were destroyed, 'through comfort whereof Thomas earl of Kildare, then being in ward within your city of Dublin, was conveyed from thence by Sir Roland fitz Eustace, knight, your treasurer of your land of Ireland, into your said county of Kildare, and so they with such following as they could make went in to the said Gerot to aid and support him'. The deputy must have been expecting trouble, for he quickly had an army in the field and finally defeated Gerot. The earl of Kildare and the treasurer then came in and were allowed to return to the king's peace. The reason given by the lords in their report was that the king's subjects 'should continue in the more tranquillity and peace' because of the influence which Kildare had over both the Irish enemies and English rebels who were 'bounden in affinity to him'. There was widespread trouble in Ulster too; in Louth and in Tipperary, Cavan and, inevitably, in Leinster. Such scattered outbreaks, while probably not collusive, must have demonstrated to both the deputy and the king how great an influence the two Geraldine earls had in Ireland. It must have come as a shock. In such a dangerous situation, Tiptoft had come to the bitter realisation that the goodwill and cooperation of Kildare was necessary if peace was to be secured. Later, in the summer, when Kildare's attainder was reversed (it was the first act of the seventh session of the same parliament which attainted him), he had to promise 'to make the Irish-men of Leinster to be at peace according to his power'.

Tiptoft retained the favour of the king after this, being retained in office and receiving gifts. So there was no question of him being made a scapegoat for a plan which had gone wrong. Kildare was biding his time. When Tiptoft was recalled to England in 1470, the Irish council, dominated by Kildare, seized the chance to elect him justiciar (even though Tiptoft had left a deputy behind him). This was the final demonstration of Geraldine influence, an expression of Anglo-Irish determination to be the masters of Ireland, and the real beginning of the ascendancy of Kildare.

6 The Kildare Ascendancy

Kildare gains control

On 2 October 1470, when Edward IV fled overseas, Henry VI was restored to rule in England. One of the first victims of the new Lancastrian government was John Tiptoft, earl of Worcester, now hated in England no less than in Ireland. On 18 October he was tried at Westminster and on the following day was beheaded on Tower Hill. His death created a vacancy in the lieutenancy of Ireland and the obvious person to fill it was the duke of Clarence, one of the leading supporters of the Lancastrian coup and the man whom Tiptoft had replaced in the Irish office. But he did not in fact become lieutenant until February 1471, and in the meantime the seventh earl of Kildare had been elected justiciar by the Irish council. When exactly that happened we do not know, but it was sometime before 13 October. It seems certain, then, that knowledge of the Lancastrian invasion of England had precipitated a crisis in Ireland, still loyal to the house of York, and that the election of Kildare to the chief governorship was designed to hold the country for Edward IV. In November 1470, at a time when the Lancastrians had assumed complete control of England, Kildare's Dublin parliament ordered a new coinage to be struck, bearing the legend 'Edward by the grace of God king of England and lord of Ireland'. The parliament itself, according to the heading of the roll of parliament, was held 'in the tenth year of the reign of King Edward IV, before Thomas fitz Morice, earl of Kildare, justiciar of the said lord the king in his land of Ireland'. Edward's kingship was thus proclaimed in the most formal manner possible.

Whatever the reason for it (and it is easy to suggest that self-interest was the only motive, though less easy to prove it), the house of Kildare remained consistently loyal to the house of York, even attempting to dethrone the first of the Tudors at the end of the fifteenth century. This attachment to York was no doubt one reason for the extraordinary rise to power in Ireland of the seventh earl of Kildare. He was, of course, the only great Anglo-Irish magnate left active in Irish political life. The earl of Desmond, after the execution of his father, sulked in the southwest and refused to participate in government. The fatal involvement of the house of Butler in Lancastrian politics, the attainder of the leading Butlers and the confiscation of their lands, removed the greatest enemies of the Geraldines. Only Kildare was left and he seized his chance. From now on, with few intervals, an earl of Kildare was to rule Ireland until Henry VIII smashed them in 1534. The eighth earl, the 'great earl' as he is commonly known, ruled under four kings (Edward IV, Richard III, Henry VII and Henry VIII) despite all attempts to remove him. The ninth earl, too, managed to hold on to office, even when English enemies tried to oust him. It was only the foolhardiness of his son, the brash young man called Silken Thomas, which brought to an end the ascendancy of Kildare.

Bases of Kildare power

The basis of the power of the Kildares was in the first place the vast landed wealth which they possessed. Their estates made them immensely wealthy and they used their control of the government to further augment their lands. For example, an act of parliament of 1482 allowed the eighth earl, 'because he did relieve and peacably bring to the king's obedience the counties of Carlow and Kildare', to occupy the lands of absentees in a great belt 'from the town of Calveston unto the castle of Carlow and on to the bridge of Leighlin'. The same earl occupied Powerscourt and settled galloglasses on lands bordering the modern Blessington lakes in Wicklow. An act of 1479 gave him the power to receive two-thirds of the rents and profits of lands held by absentees, supposedly for the defence of the land of peace, but in practice to be expended by the earl in his own interests as he saw fit. Early in the sixteenth century he was given a grant of all lands which he could recover from rebels, a privilege which naturally encouraged him to be at war as often as it might lead to a recovery of lands. This extraordinary privilege was passed on to his son after his death.

Control of parliament, through the council, was vital to the Kildares. It enabled them to augment their own power, to dispense patronage, reward dependants, and look after their own interests. The parliament of 1470, for instance, permitted the heir of the seventh earl, whenever his father should die, to have livery of all his inheritance without any delay. In 1478, parliament rewarded Kildare supporters, such as Sir Roland fitz Eustace and James Ketyng, the prior of Kilmainham. The following year parliament empowered the earl to exempt people from the act of resumption which had been passed at an earlier session. This gave Kildare a great power of rewarding friends or punishing enemies. A later act constituted the Fraternity of Arms which, as we shall see, became yet another instrument of Kildare power. The twenty-ninth act reduced the rate at which the earl's manor of Moylagh in Meath was to be assessed for subsidies and the forty-first act made Conn O Neill (who had recently married the earl's sister Eleanor) to be 'of free estate and free condition in the law, as the king's liegeman; and that the said Conn and his issue begotten and to be begotten between the said Conn and Eleanor, be adjudged English'.

This marriage alliance with O Neill, which led to a military alliance, was typical of the manner in which the earl fashioned a network of relationships with the great Gaelic and Anglo-Irish families of Ireland. His daughter Margaret married Piers Butler, later earl of Ormond; Elizabeth was married to Christopher Fleming of Slane; and Alice to Conn O Neill, later earl of Tyrone (and son of Eleanor, the earl's sister); Eustacia was married to Burke of Clanricard; Joan to O Carroll of Ely; a son Oliver married Maeve O Connor of Offaly; another, Richard, to Maud Darcy; a third, Walter, to Elizabeth Plunket, daughter of Lord Dunsany. Naturally these marriages often made it possible for the earl to employ Gaelic or Anglo-Irish lords in one capacity or another, a striking example being the large army which the earl was able to bring together before the battle of Knockdoe in 1505. But not all marriages resulted in an alliance of friendship – the opposition at Knockdoe centred on that same Clanricard to whom the earl's daughter Eustacia was married. Allies had to be bought and maintained with favours, or else forced by their need of protection into dependence on the earl.

The Kildare Rental, begun in 1518, shows the extraordinary range of Kildare power and influence. A section entitled 'Duties upon Irishmen' lists the Gaelic lordships which were paying annual fees to the earl for protection. The Mac Murroughs, O Tooles, O Byrnes, O Mores, O Connors, O Farrells, O Reillys are only some of the great names listed, each paying a fee, sometimes in kind – O Dwyer, for example, sent a nest of goshawks; Mac Mahon supplied a small force of seven 'sparrys' (spears). A most interesting feature of some of them is the clear statement that payment is conditional on the earl being in office as deputy; in others, payment is to be reduced by half if the earl should not be in office. Nothing could show more clearly the importance to the earl of holding office, for the power it gave him. Nor is it anything less than extraordinary that it should be taken for granted that an earl of Kildare would normally hold the office of deputy, almost as an hereditary possession.

An interesting survival from 1530 shows clearly what the purpose of these 'duties' was. It is an agreement in Irish between the ninth earl and the Mac Rannells (Reynolds) of Leitrim, stipulating that a shilling from the rent in every quarter of land is to be paid to the earl at All Hallows every year, 'in consideration of the earl's defending and assisting them against all men subject to his authority'. The earl was acting outside the law in levying such exactions though it was long since a blind eye was turned to such practices in many parts of the lordship. For the earl was by no means unique. It is evident that other great Anglo-Irish lords, such as the earls of Desmond, or the Burkes, or the earl of Ossory, were also engaged in offering 'protection' in return for annual fees. A report in 1534, addressed to the king, described the situation bluntly: 'For the more part all the captains of the wild Irish is in subjection and doth bear great tribute to your said earls'. Only in this way could some kind of equilibrium be maintained, at no cost to the king but greatly to the advantage of the great magnates.

The earls of Kildare were able to call on considerable military reserves, which made them powerful friends or adversaries. They never lost an opportunity of augmenting their military strength and the creation of a Fraternity of Arms (later the Guild of St George) by the Dublin parliament of 1474 supplied them with a small standing army of 120 mounted archers, 40 horsemen and 40 pages. The justification for setting up this force was that 'this land of Ireland is greatly wasted and destroyed as well by the king's Irish enemies as by English rebels by reason that no continual resistance is or hitherto has been ordained and provided for the defence of the same'. This was true. Now that English chief governors with small armies were no longer being sent to Ireland regularly, there was a genuine need for a standing army of some sort. But the original brotherhood of thirteen 'of the most honourable and loyally disposed persons' were Kildare supporters and the earl himself was elected captain of the army. That it was used as an instrument of Kildare policy is certain. When William Sherwood, the bishop of Meath and a bitter enemy of the house of Kildare, became deputy, he abolished poundage (on which the Fraternity depended to maintain its army) in his parliament of 1477 and thus effectively dissolved the army controlled by Kildare. When Kildare was restored to office, he had poundage revived and the Fraternity reestablished. When some of the original Fraternity ceased to be Kildare supporters (such as Sir Robert Eustace or Robert Dowdall), they were replaced by loyal men like Sir Nicholas Wogan, James Ketyng, prior of Kilmainham, or John Fleming, baron of Slane, with whom Kildare had made a marriage alliance. The Fraternity of Arms was clearly a Geraldine guild.

Control of office

Ultimately, however, the position of Kildare in Irish politics rested on his ability to dominate the Irish council. This in effect meant that he had to control the important ministers who sat in council *ex officio*. He could only exercise control if he held the power of appointment and dismissal, something which no king could easily hand over to his chief governor since it made him virtually uncheckable, especially since he was already not accountable for the revenues he received. But for many years the Kildares held this power in practice, sometimes in open defiance of the expressed wishes of the king. In his Naas parliament of 1472, the earl saw to it that his earlier appointments were confirmed 'by authority of the said parliament' and, by way of safeguarding his right to appoint in the future, had it 'ordained and established that all offices which shall become vacant in this land, in whatsoever manner it shall happen, the said deputy may give and grant the said offices and every of them to any person or persons for term of life years or otherwise'. A notorious example occurred in 1483, when Kildare refused to admit Robert St Laurence to the office of chancellor, despite the fact that he had no less than three separate patents of appointment from Edward IV, Edward V and Richard III. Kildare had already appointed his brother, Thomas fitz Gerald, to the office and he refused to dismiss him. The whole thing came to a climax when Kildare received a letter from the king, written in December 1483, which ordered him, 'in the straitest wise possible', to admit Howth to office 'without any further delay or disputation of our interest' and which threatened, in the event of the deputy refusing to comply, to dismiss him from office and to 'provide for such a governance there as shall not presume to deroge, argue or diminish our power royal or prerogative'. But it was Thomas who remained in office, despite all that the king could threaten, and Kildare retained the deputyship.

In his letter Richard III referred to the Statute of Henry fitz Empress, which supposedly conferred authority on the chief governor of Ireland to fill a vacancy in the offices of chancellor or treasurer: '. . . surmising that ye have sufficient authority to do so by reason of certain old privileges granted to the justice of our said land by our noble progenitor Henry fitz Empress, sometime king of England, and by other kings his successors authorised and confirmed'. Earlier references support the existence of a custom, based on a mythical statute of Henry II (fitz Empress), empowering the chief governor to make such appointments. But the most important provision of the 'statute' related to the filling of a vacancy in the office of chief governor itself. A famous act of the parliament summoned by Kildare in 1485 confirmed the 'statute' of Henry fitz Empress, 'ordained for the election of the chief governor to be had in this land at any time it shall happen to be without any legal governor'.

It went on to list the members of the council who *ex officio* were to form a college of electors, and having named the individuals, it stipulated that they were to retain their offices for life. In the event of any of them vacating office, the replacement was to be in the gift of Kildare.

The failure of Lord Grey

As we shall see, this was Kildare's way of ensuring that he would remain in office even with a change of dynasty in England, a contingency that was very possible in the summer of 1485. But he and his father had long since managed to learn how to survive crises of that kind. A most notable example of the earl's ability to hang onto office, and more or less on his own terms, is provided by the intrusion of Lord Grey in 1478. In the early months of that year, because of the attainder of the king's brother Clarence, lieutenant of Ireland, the post of deputy became vacant. The Irish council proceeded to elect the seventh earl of Kildare to fill the vacancy in early March and when he died shortly afterwards, his son, the eighth earl, was immediately elected to fill his place. The important thing about the council which made these elections is that it was composed solely of the seven leading ministers, all firm supporters of Kildare. When the king, through his appointment of Grey as deputy, tried to undermine Kildare's control of the Irish government, it is significant that the new deputy added a strong non-ministerial element to the council as an elective body. In any case, after his election Kildare summoned a parliament, which had sessions at Naas, Dublin and Connell in county Kildare in May, July and September. But in July, after the first session, Grey was appointed by the king. The sequel was an extraordinary demonstration of Kildare's power in Ireland. First of all the earl and the council refused to accept the validity of Grey's appointment because it was made under the king's privy seal. Roland fitz Eustace, who held jointly the offices of treasurer and chancellor, refused access to the great seal, so that Grey found it impossible to govern until a new seal could be provided. The treasurer also assigned all the revenues (nominally at the disposal of the deputy), so that nothing was left for Grey. James Ketyng, who had been given custody of Dublin castle by Kildare, despite a grant of it to another for life by the king, refused to admit the new deputy into the castle and even broke down the drawbridge to prevent access. Worst of all, Kildare's parliament met in session again and passed a series of statutes.

The king could not stand idly by and watch his chief governor flouted in this way. Grey, too, had held a parliament which met late in the year and continued into 1479, with sessions at Trim, Drogheda and Dublin. This parliament proceeded to squash the statutes of Kildare's parliament, upheld the legitimacy of Grey's appointment, and enacted a series of statutes of its own. One of these, on the excuse that there was doubt as to how a justiciar should be elected to fill a vacancy, enacted that the electorate in future should consist of the whole council, with the archbishops of Armagh and Dublin, and the bishops of Meath and Kildare, the mayors of Drogheda and Dublin, and all the lords, spiritual and temporal, of the four counties of Dublin, Louth, Meath and Kildare. By the time this parliament had finished its work, the king was fully informed of the Irish situation – two rival parliaments with two sets of contradictory statutes, and his deputy being refused recognition by the most important section of the community. It was time to intervene. Both Grey and Kildare crossed over to England and appeared before Edward. Whatever was said during the discussion, Kildare emerged the victor. Grey was dismissed and the earl appointed deputy in his place. The king also gave him a series of instructions, subsequently enrolled on the Irish close roll, expressing his 'will, determination, commandment and pleasure upon the parliament held late at the Naas and

Drogheda and upon the parliament that shall be next held within his land of Ireland'. These 'instructions' are an important anticipation of the later enactment known as Poynings' Law, which provided that all bills must first be approved by the king and council in England before being introduced into parliament in Ireland. Indeed, Edward IV went further, for he was actually initiating legislation. But although Kildare was careful to introduce some of the proposed legislation in his next parliament, he omitted one very important act which might have damaged his own interests. The king had commanded that 'such an act as heretofore hath been made in the land there restraining that no man within that land shall be called out of the said land by any precept or commandment made under the king's great seal, privy seal, or signet in England be utterly revoked and annulled'. This referred to an act of the famous parliament of 1460, held before his father the duke of York. But Kildare ignored this instruction and let the act stand.

In the indenture between the king and Kildare, which fixed the terms of his appointment, it was agreed that he should have a small army of 80 'yeomen, able archers' and 40 'other horsemen, called spears'. To provide for the cost of this it was settled that the deputy should have £600 annually from the revenues of Ireland. But, should the Irish revenues not be able to meet this charge, the money was to be supplied from England. With fitz Eustace as treasurer, no longer held to account in England, it was an easy matter for Kildare to see to it that the £600 became a charge on England – an extra bonus which made control of the deputyship even more worthwhile.

For the rest of the reign Edward IV and Kildare seem to have got on well enough. The earl must have had a powerful personality. He certainly made a deep impression on Henry VII later. We can only presume that his meeting with Edward IV in 1479 convinced the king that there was no point in trying to govern Ireland without the earl. Kildare had proved to be indispensable. For his part, the earl made every effort to keep the king content. He made a present of a horse, called 'Bayard Kyldare', in 1481, which the king shortly afterwards gave to the brother of the king of Scotland. But Edward IV died in April 1483 and in the following June his brother became king as Richard III. Immediately Kildare found himself faced with someone who was determined to regain control of Ireland.

Richard III and Kildare

Richard III began his reign on 26 June. Three weeks later he appointed his eldest son Edward lieutenant of Ireland and late in the same month of July he sent William Lacy on a mission to Ireland. Lacy was given 'instructions' which show clearly that the main purpose of his embassy was to persuade Kildare to remain as deputy, though on the king's terms. He was to hold office under contract for a period of one year and thereafter at the king's pleasure. Lacy was to persuade the earl to come to England to seal an indenture of service. All other ministers were to hold office at the king's pleasure. These proposals would have ended Kildare's monopoly of government and they show the king's desire, right at the outset of his reign, to regain control of Ireland. He announced that next in importance to the 'establishment of this his realm of England, principally afore other things intendeth for the weal of this land of Ireland to set and advise such good rule and politic guiding there as any of his noble progenitors have done or intended in times past to reduce it'. He also made it known that he planned to come to Ireland in person, 'whensoever he may have first leisure thereunto', to relieve the land 'by his immediate authority'. He also asked for a statement of Irish revenues, the first time such a request had come from an English king for generations.

Behind this display of determination on the part of the king lay the unpalatable fact that at least for the immediate future he needed Kildare to govern Ireland. Nor did he have much success in his attempts to enforce the principle that all important ministers must hold office at the king's pleasure. So much is clear from the letter of December 1483 which we quoted, in which the king rebuked Kildare for refusing to admit Lord Howth to office as chancellor, and from the legislation of the 1485 parliament which confirmed the present ministers in office for life and gave Kildare the right to replace them during vacancy. Before that happened, Kildare had sent John Estrete to the king with replies to the messages brought to Ireland by Lacy. In these replies Kildare showed his strength. He excused his failure to come to England, implying that he feared for his safety and requesting a guarantee of safe conduct under the seals of some of the great lords of England; he requested office for ten years, a stipend of £1,000, a grant of the manor of Leixlip, and custody of the castle of Wicklow. There was a hint of menace in the secret instructions which were given to Estrete, to stress to the king the influence which the earl exercised through his 'children, brethren, kin and allies'.

The sparring continued, as is clear from the reply sent to Kildare. It requested that he come to the king by the following 1 August (Richard adding that he 'marveleth that he can desire any promises, seals, or writings of any of his lords more that of his grace only') and he will 'enlarge' the grant of office to ten years. A statement of Irish revenues was again requested (which in fact was later sent and which showed that most of the revenues had either been alienated or regularly assigned, so that only about £180 was available to the governor), so that arrangements might be made to pay a stipend to Kildare. The earl duly went to the king in August, when most of his demands were met. His power in Ireland, then, continued unabated.

But Richard III was soon demanding his price. He had plans for Ulster (the earldom was his) and he wished

Kildare to use his influence with his brother-in-law O Neill, who 'hath and occupieth most part thereof', to persuade him to accept the king's favour and livery. He was also to bring O Donnell back to his allegiance and he, 'the Plunkets or any lord or noble man of that land, borderer or other' were to do the best they could in aid of the king's intentions.

At the same time the king was preparing the way towards freeing himself from dependence on Kildare. His emissary, the bishop of Annaghdown, also contacted the earl of Desmond. He was to be told that although his father was 'slain and murdered by colour of the laws . . . against all manhood, reason and good conscience' when Richard III was young, the king 'always continueth and hath inward compassion of the death of his said father'. A collar of gold was given to Desmond, who was then requested to return to the king's allegiance. A present of clothing was also sent, so that the earl might give up the Irish dress he sported and return to English ways. The king also promised to find him a suitable wife. But in the event Desmond clung to his Gaelic way of life and married the daughter of Tadhg O Brien. The bishop, however, had letters for a number of other Anglo-Irish lords, not only in Munster but in Connacht as well and it seems clear that the king was trying to establish direct relations with families such as the Powers, and thus break through the restrictions of Kildare's influence.

Richard was never given the chance to develop this line of policy. Already, at the end of 1483, Henry Tudor had been proclaimed king at Rennes and before very long was to win the English Crown. Kildare knew well what was in the wind and with a change of dynasty possible in England began to safeguard his position in Ireland. As we saw, an act of parliament on 6 June 1485 'confirmed, ratified and made good and effectual in law' the mythical statute fitz Empress. Thus Kildare was safe in the event of an emergency brought about by the sudden accession of Henry Tudor in England. More than that, it confirmed the seven chief ministers, all firm supporters of Kildare, in office for life and gave those seven control over the election of a justiciar. Kildare thus secured his continuity in office and not a minute too soon, for at the end of August the battle of Bosworth gave Henry the Crown.

Accession of Henry VII

The new king had more than enough to contend with in England to worry much about the position in Ireland. Kildare was an unknown quantity, however, with the long family tradition of loyalty to the house of York. By contrast, the Butlers had long been supporters of Lancaster, and Henry now proceeded to restore the earldom of Ormond to Thomas Butler, younger brother of the earl of Wiltshire who had been executed in 1461. This must have seriously alarmed Kildare, who had recently taken the precaution of marrying his daughter Margaret to Sir Piers Butler in Ireland, the same man who had been given the 'custody and defence' of the lands of the earldom in Ireland. The return of the Butlers to favour in England, the fear that Henry might in time try to rid himself of Kildare (despite reappointing him deputy in March 1486) and perhaps, too, a genuine belief in the right of the house of York to rule England – all this may have been responsible for the dangerous step taken by Kildare early in 1487, when he became heavily involved in a plot to dethrone the king.

Lambert Simnel

Richard Simmons, an Oxford priest, arrived in Dublin with a young boy, Lambert Simnel, son of an obscure Oxford tradesman. He claimed to be Edward, earl of Warwick, son of the duke of Clarence, true heir to the English throne. The real earl was in fact a prisoner in the Tower of London; but, for whatever reason, the imposter was enthusiastically accepted as genuine by the Anglo-Irish (with some few exceptions), including Kildare. He was lodged in Dublin castle, proclaimed Edward VI, king of England, and on 24 May was solemnly crowned in Christ Church cathedral. All of this was bad enough. But worse was the plot, hatched abroad, to provide an army with which the pretender could invade England from Ireland. The earl of Lincoln, who had been nominated his heir by Richard III shortly before his death, fled to Flanders and there, with other disaffected Yorkists, began preparations to depose King Henry. An army of 2,000 German mercenaries, under the command of Martin Schwarz, was brought to Ireland by Lincoln in early May. In June England was invaded. It is not known how many Irishmen joined the invasion, but all the literary evidence suggests that large numbers were led by Kildare's brother, Thomas. The earl himself wisely remained at home in the security of Ireland. Subsequently, in mid-June, the battle of Stoke saw the defeat of the pretender's army. According to one description of the battle, the Irish were slain in droves, 'like dull and brute beasts'. Simnel was taken prisoner and was made a servant in the royal kitchen.

The plot had come to nothing in the end, but it made Henry aware of the potential danger of Ireland. Kildare was still holding out for the Yorkists there and he certainly had not submitted as late as 20 October, four months after the defeat at Stoke. It was not until 25 May 1488, just one year after he had Simnel crowned, that a pardon was made out for Kildare. He was the most important of a long list of Irishmen, clerical as well as lay, for whom pardons were made out on that day. He must have made known his intention of making submission by then, for already preparations were under way for the mission of Sir Richard Edgecombe to Ireland. He was to receive the submission of all the rebels during the summer.

Edgecombe's mission is in itself a clear indication that

however frightened Henry may have been by seeing Ireland once again the focus of a Yorkist plot, he could not afford to deal harshly with Kildare and the other Anglo-Irish. With only four ships and a small number of men (he couldn't have had anything like the 500 traditionally assigned to him in what was clearly a naval and not a land force), Edgecombe could hardly expect to be able to force reluctant rebels into submission. During the course of the mission, Kildare's supreme confidence was well demonstrated. He treated Edgecombe with obvious contempt – he kept him waiting for over a month in Dublin, while he went on pilgrimage; when he finally came, he had 200 mounted soldiers with him and instead of going to the king's ambassador, he ordered Edgecombe to come to him, receiving him in great state in St. Thomas Court. He and the other Anglo-Irish refused to accept the conditions laid down by the king for their submissions, notably certain sanctions (involving the forfeiture of estates in the event of future rebellion) to guarantee their good behaviour in the future. It was on that occasion, according to the narrative of Edgecombe's voyage, that the earl and the council made the famous declaration that 'rather than they would do it, they would become Irish every one of them'. Subsequently, Kildare retired to his castle at Maynooth and eventually Edgecombe had to follow him there. Long drawn-out discussions followed, with Kildare and his supporters refusing to budge. Edgecombe had to give away. Kildare and the others eventually took an oath of loyalty on 21 July and received their pardons.

A letter from the archbishop of Armagh, Octavian del Palatio, who was one of the very few to remain loyal to the king during the period of the Simnel plot, said: 'I know for certain that if it should come to pass that the aforesaid earl of Kildare obtain the governorship of Ireland by royal authority and appoints the chancellor of Ireland at his own pleasure, I have no hope of peace in Ireland'. But the king really had no choice but to fall back on Kildare again. The alternative was to return to the old and expensive policy of royal intervention, employing a military chief governor with a small army. This Henry was not prepared to do. It was the appearance of another pretender in Ireland, with the emergence of yet another Yorkist plot against him there, and the ambiguous (to say the least) attitude of Kildare, which forced his hand.

Perkin Warbeck

In November 1491 John Taylor, known to be Yorkist and plotting against the king, landed in Cork. He had with him a youth, Perkin Warbeck, who claimed to be Richard second son of Edward IV. He was received with enthusiasm by the citizens and the mayor, the latter standing by him until both were executed in 1499. Cork seems to have been chosen because Warbeck hoped to get support from the earl of Desmond, which indeed was forthcoming. He also claimed later to have been helped by Kildare, though the earl strongly denied this in a letter he wrote in February 1493: 'I never lay with him, nor aided, comforted, nor supported him, with goods nor in no other manner wise'. Kildare's involvement with Warbeck is impossible to prove. But as deputy, he seems to have done nothing to counter the activities of the plotters in Ireland and his attitude may well have been at best only neutral. At any rate the suspicions of the king were soon aroused. He had ordered Kildare to England in the summer of 1490, sending a pardon of a technical breach of statutes against giving liveries and keeping retinues, on condition that the earl travel within ten months. Kildare let the long interval expire and then got the Irish council to write to Henry that his presence in Ireland was absolutely indispensable, because of the state of the country. He wrote himself, saying that one special reason why he was detained in Ireland was that he had been called in to settle a dispute between his cousin,

Desmond, and Burke of Connacht. Finally, again at his instigation, Desmond and three others wrote from Limerick, repeating the same excuse and adding that they feared that the north might be destroyed in his absence and that they were worried because of the dangers he might encounter in travelling to and fro across the sea.

Excuses of this kind must have given Henry cause for worry, which turned to alarm at the suspicion that Kildare was involved in another Yorkist plot in the winter of 1491. He effectively dismissed him from office in December and replaced him in June 1492 by Walter fitz Simmons, archbishop of Dublin. At the same time, Kildare supporters were removed from office and Alexander Plunket became chancellor, with James Ormond (a bastard son of the fifth earl) as treasurer.

James Ormond was already in Ireland. In December 1491, he and Thomas Garth led an army to suppress a rebellion in Kilkenny and Tipperary, which does not seem to have had any connexion with the Warbeck plot. He was also attorney of the absentee earl of Ormond and his vigorous attempts to reassert Ormond's rights not only stirred up trouble with Piers Butler (with whom Kildare was now allied by marriage), but caused the old Butler-Geraldine quarrel to break out again. Faction fights were frequent. A famous story relates how during one such fight in the streets of Dublin, when some houses were burned, James was pursued by Kildare himself, until he took refuge in the chapter-house of St Patrick's. Fearing for his life, he barred himself in and would accept no guarantee of his safety. A hole was cut in the door, so that he and Kildare could shake hands. But James was still afraid, until the earl finally put his hand through and peace was made between them.

By now accusations against Kildare began to reach the king, serious enough to make him decide to go over to England to answer the different charges in person. He must have been confident of his ability to carry the day, a confidence which is reflected in the famous *Book of Howth* description of the meeting between himself and Henry VII. He supposedly treated the king on equal terms, making ribald jokes at the expense of his main accuser, his old enemy, the bishop of Meath. At length, the bishop could contain himself no longer: 'You see the sort of man he is; all Ireland cannot rule him'. To which Henry is supposed to have made the well-known reply: 'No? Then he must be the man to rule all Ireland'. And according to the story, he reappointed him deputy and sent him back to govern Ireland.

But the reality behind the story was very different. The earl did manage to gain the favour of the king, who gave him in marriage to his own first cousin, Elizabeth St John, with a huge dowry. He also appointed him deputy. But that was in August 1496. Not until then did the king think it safe to allow Kildare to govern Ireland again. And in the meantime he had tried to revolutionise the administration, making it English in personnel and directly responsible to himself. It is notable that from now on, with the exception of Poynings in 1494, the governors of Ireland were unable to appoint or dismiss the chief ministers. And in the meantime, Henry had overhauled the revenues of Ireland, attempted to reform the financial administration, sent Poynings with an army to prevent Warbeck from continuing to use Ireland as a base, and by means of the famous Poynings' Law, ended the independence of the medieval Irish parliament. Danger was thus averted and Kildare could come back.

King Henry intervenes

That there was danger in Ireland had been made plain by the Lambert Simnel affair and by the continued flirting of some of the Anglo-Irish and Gaelic Irish with Perkin Warbeck. Henry tried to meet this danger by the kind of military and political action which would not involve him in heavy and sustained expenditure. The small expedition of 200, which came under the command of James Ormond and Thomas Garth in the winter of 1491, cost him only £800. This seems to have been sufficient to contain Warbeck in Ireland and in the spring of 1492 he left for France. But, as we saw, the activities of James Ormond in Kilkenny and Tipperary, aided by O Brien, stirred up old Butler-Geraldine rivalries and resulted in faction fights. Rival groups came to blows in the streets of Dublin; Ormond, aided by Garth, raided Offaly, the territory of the O Connor ally of Kildare; Garth was taken prisoner by Kildare, who reputedly hanged his son. So, with Ireland in turmoil again, Henry had to send another army in March 1493. It was led by Sir Roger Cotton and numbered 200. Ordnance as well as £240 in ready cash was brought, and three wagon loads of munitions, including barrels of powder for the cannon, were sent on. Another captain, Henry Mountford, brought an extra 100 men; and later, in June, Henry Wyatt brought a force which was just short of 100. The total brought, then, came to around 400 and cost £2,825 in 1493. The cost of Ireland was mounting.

The faction fights continued. A famous incident in Oxmantown Green in Dublin in June 1493 saw a former mayor and two citizens killed by Geraldine supporters. The new administration mounted its attack on Kildare. In the Dublin parliament in the summer of 1493, a massive act of resumption from Henry VI was clearly designed to get at the earl and his supporters. Another act required the late treasurer, Roland fitz Eustace, Kildare's father-in-law, to account for the impossibly long period of forty years during which he had been treasurer. It was then that Kildare went to England, followed by James Ormond, the new deputy (Gormanston) and others. In March 1494 Desmond took an oath of fealty ('I shall be faithful subject and true liegeman unto our said sovereign lord'), though he inserted a revealing proviso that he could not promise to appear before a lieutenant or deputy 'unless I think that safely from thence again I may depart', for fear he should be mistreated 'as my father have been'. The memory of the judicial murder of the earl of Desmond was still very much alive and clearly any pledge of Desmond's was not going to be of much real value. In May Kildare, in an indenture with the king, promised to keep Desmond to his pledge.

The mission of Poynings

It was now, possibly advised by all the important people from Ireland who had gathered in England, that Henry VII decided to make a decisive intervention in Ireland. He appointed Edward Poynings as deputy on 12 September 1494, with Hugh Conway as treasurer and Henry Deane as chancellor. Other appointments of new men to office in Ireland had been made in August. An army of about 430 was mobilised, arms and artillery gathered, and ready cash provided. All of this was in fulfilment of Henry's determination to send 'a good and sufficient army accompanied by good and great persons as well for war as for justice'. This was how he expressed it in a communication to the king of France on 10 August. Now that England was at peace, he had decided to pacify Ireland, especially the parts inhabited by 'Irish savages', who were to be brought under English law. It may be true that Henry was genuine in his ambition, since he sent Kildare and James Ormond back with Poynings and clearly expected full cooperation from both of them. And the proposed thorough reform of the administration, employing trusted officials of his own chamber, indicated that this was no mere military intervention. But even with Geraldine support, he could hardly have expected Poynings and his army of 400 (plus the 100 or so which Garth still commanded) to conquer Ireland. It is much more likely, then, that it was fear of Warbeck which made the king take Ireland in hand, a fear which is clearly indicated in a secret communication to France, which shows Henry's anxiety to make sure that the pretender would receive no help there. Already Warbeck had been recognised as king of England by the Emperor Maximilian, and it was common knowledge that he was preparing an expedition to invade England. A landing was expected at any time and given the continuing Yorkist sympathies of sections of the Munster Anglo-Irish, and the known involvement of O Donnell in Donegal with the king of Scots, who was also backing Warbeck, it is hardly surprising that Henry was worried lest England should once again be invaded by way of Ireland. It was the mission of Poynings to prevent this happening.

As soon as he arrived in Ireland, the deputy moved northwards. Accompanied by Kildare, James Ormond, and an army considerably less than 1,000, he seems to have been aiming at preventing collusion between O Donnell, Warbeck and Scotland. But he got no further than the country of O Hanlon in Armagh, when a bitter quarrel between himself and Kildare brought the campaign to an end. The origin of the quarrel is unknown, though it may be that the earl was violently opposed to the destructive tactics of the deputy and especially James Ormond, which ruined tracts of O Hanlon's lands and those of his ally Hugh Magennis of Down. Kildare was later arrested, in February 1496, and was attainted of treason in an Irish parliament. The main charge against him was that he tried to promote war against the deputy and, more specifically, 'conspired with the king's Irish enemies to have murdered and slain the said deputy in the said O Hanlon's country at the time of his being there'. But depositions from both O Hanlon and Magennis in 1496, as a result of which the attainder of Kildare was reversed, make it clear that he advised the two lords to make their peace with Poynings, despite the fact that (in the words of Magennis) 'he has destroyed my land and property completely, and he cannot do me more harm than he has done, so I may as well war with him as peace'.

After his arrest and attainder, in the spring of 1495, Kildare was sent as a prisoner to England. A Geraldine rebellion followed, in which Carlow castle was taken by the earl's brother, James. This engaged Poynings and diverted him from the north. Then, in July, the long-awaited Warbeck invasion materialised. He and his small fleet appeared off Munster and then, joined by Desmond, laid siege to Waterford. All available forces were mustered to meet the threat. The Dublin Assembly, for example, enacted no ordinances after 24 June, because (the record tells us) 'the mayor, bailiffs and divers of the Commons were at Waterford in Munster with Sir Edward Poynings'. By August the siege was lifted, mainly because of Poynings' efficient use of artillery. Warbeck, with the help of Shane Burke, O Donnell and O Neill of Clandeboy, made his way through Connacht to Donegal and thence to Scotland. He no longer represented a real threat to Henry VII and this was made clear in January 1496, when Henry was unconditionally invited to join the Holy League by its founder Maximilian.

Poynings did not leave Ireland until December 1495, by which time he had organised a system of defence around the Pale. The army had been split into a large number of small forces and these were distributed around the area. A warning system of fires on various hills was devised. Trenches were dug. The situation seemed to be well under control. By the summer the army was drastically reduced in size and the Geraldine rebellion was coming to an end. In July Kildare's brother James made his peace – Desmond had already made terms and had taken an oath of allegiance on 15 March. It was now safe to consider letting Kildare back to Ireland.

Financial reform

The real measure of Henry VII's fear of Yorkist plots in Ireland is the amount of money he spent in meeting the threat. Between 1491 and 1496 about £23,000 was spent on armies in Ireland. But the great bulk of this, something over £18,000, went during the Poynings intervention and down to the disbanding of the army in the summer of 1496. Henry couldn't afford this level of expenditure. Not surprisingly, therefore, he tried to improve the finances of Ireland, a task entrusted to the 'new men' (associated with the chamber), who were the great buttress of the new Tudor rule in England. Associated with the treasurer, Hugh Conway, were two special commissioners, Henry Wyatt and William Hattecliffe, who made a thorough survey of the Irish revenues, prepared detailed estimates of receipts, and generally tried to make collection and accounting more efficient and productive. The terms of Conway's appointment gave the treasurer increased powers, while at the same time bringing him within range of the English accounting system. In the century or so after the great financial reforms of the 1290s, the treasurer of Ireland was regularly summoned to Westminster to have his accounts audited. This provided an important check on the Irish government, more especially after the chief governor was freed from the necessity of rendering accounts. Even in the fifteenth century, when such summonses were only intermittently issued, the practice was not allowed to drop. However, after the audit of Giles Thorndon's account in 1446, no other treasurer was summoned to England. It is significant that he was the last of the English officials to be appointed to the office of treasurer for many years and there can be no doubt that the stranglehold which the Anglo-Irish, and especially Kildare, gained on the government was responsible for this. Thorndon himself had protested, without avail, against the alienation of royal revenues in Ireland. It is important, therefore, that the terms of Conway's appointment in 1494 made mandatory a declaration of accounts, which was to be certified in the English exchequer.

In the event, the attempted financial reforms achieved very little, though for the first time for years a large (by Irish standards) surplus of about £500 was produced. But it was clear that no administrative reform at this juncture was going to produce the kind of money necessary to maintain an adequate army in Ireland. By 1496, for example, it cost £294.11.1 a month to keep an army of 330 Englishmen, 100 kernes and one trumpeter in Ireland. So Henry gave up the attempt. In the meantime, he had faced up to the possibility that he would have to fall back on Kildare, or someone like him. This meant that he had to institute some measure of control and so he gave Poynings explicit and detailed instructions on legislation which he wished to see enacted in an Irish parliament. The composition of the new Irish council, now largely English and ministerial in personnel, made it easy enough to guarantee the passage of the necessary legislation through parliament.

Not long after he arrived, Poynings summoned his parliament which met, significantly enough, at Drogheda on 1 December 1494 and remained in session until the following March. The early acts clearly reveal the king's determination to exercise as much direct control as possible over the government of Ireland. The sixth act stipulated that all the chief ministers and 'all officers accountant, shall have their offices solely at the king's will and pleasure'. This, the act stated, was because of the 'great and manifold inconveniences that late were attempted contrary to all national allegiance' by the grant of office to some ministers for life – an obvious reference to the monopoly of office held by Kildare supporters. The next act annulled the 'pretensed prescription' of York's 1460 parliament, which made it high treason to attack any person in Ireland under an English seal; it also enacted that the great seal of England, the privy seal and signet were to be obeyed in Ireland. It is the ninth act containing Poynings' Law which is most famous: no parliament is to be held in Ireland until the proposed acts have been approved by the king and English council and the royal licence to summon a parliament procured. The eleventh act was a really horrific act of resumption, going back to Edward II. Although, as usual, a number of exceptions were made to the act, it is significant that the number is much smaller than usual and only for specific grants. Some were inserted afterwards, by the king himself and in his own hand, a sure sign that the act was a threat, designed to coerce the weaker into voting the way the king wished in parliament. Two other acts have a particular constitutional significance: the twenty-sixth effectively annulled the statute fitz Empress and the thirty-ninth provided that 'all statutes late made within the realm of England . . . shall from henceforth be deemed good and effectual in law and be accepted, used and executed within this land of Ireland'. This was intended to clear up any doubts there might have been concerning the application of English statutes to Ireland.

That Henry VII was thus attempting to provide constitutional checks on the future governors of Ireland is corroborated by the 'articles which the earl of Kildare . . . faithfully hath promised and also solemnly sworn upon the holy Evangelies to observe, keep and execute within the king's land of Ireland' in August 1496. First among these articles are the provisions of Poynings' Law and the promise to deliver rebels or traitors in reply to writs out of England. The king considered these the primary safeguards before reappointing Kildare as deputy.

The return of Kildare

Kildare, his new wife and 'all his company' landed at Howth on 17 September. On the 21st he took the oath of office in Drogheda. And on the same day, as we learn from a letter written by a royal agent in Dublin at the end of October, 'all the great Irishmen of the north parts of

Ireland had their messengers ready attending there on my lord deputy to treat of peace'. The king had not miscalculated in restoring Kildare to office. His agent reported that all the Irish of the south and west, with the exception of Mac Murrough and O Connor, were also submitting, as well as the leading adherents of Warbeck, Desmond and Shane Burke. 'Now thanked be God', he wrote, 'the king hath peace in all the land without strake or any great charge or cost to him'. He paid a handsome tribute to Kildare at the end of his letter: 'His grace could have put no man in authority here that in so short a space and with so little cost could have set this land in so good order as it is now but this man only. I trust the king shall have a great treasure of him'.

The restoration of Kildare, then, suited all parties. He could pacify the country at little cost to the king and provided that he posed no threat to the security of the Tudor dynasty, Henry was content to let him go his own way in Ireland. For reasons of economy the king had to withdraw not only his army from Ireland, but many of the personnel of the new administration as well. It was inevitable, then, that once he was back in office Kildare should regain most of his former control, despite the legislation of Poynings' parliament. For example, many strategic castles fell into his hands, although parliament had enacted that only Englishmen were to be constables of some of them; and the exactions of coyne and livery, and other similar abuses which had been condemned, were continued. The king's acquiescence in all this is clear. Kildare's first parliament, held in 1498 under Poynings' Law, restored the usage of the statute fitz Empress, although the electorate was to consist of the lords spiritual and temporal of the four shires. When Henry VII died, and the office of deputy fell vacant as a result, Kildare immediately summoned a council and then the lords of the four shires elected him justiciar.

Kildare continued to enjoy the favour of the king. In 1503 he went to England and Henry allowed his son Gerald, long a hostage, to return home, loading him with gifts of rich clothing. The following year Gerald, although only seventeen, was appointed treasurer of Ireland by the king. As long as he was able to protect the Pale, the earl could hold his own. This, on the whole, he did successfully. Small wonder that a later generation believed that the best road to success was open rebellion. A report to Cromwell in 1533 quotes a statement of Sir Gerald Mac Shane to the earl's son Thomas: 'Thou fool, thou shalt be the more esteemed in Ireland to take part against the king; for what hadst thou been if they father had not done so? What was he set by until he crowned a king here; took Garth, the king's captain prisoner; hanged his son; resisted Poynings and all deputies; killed them of Dublin upon Oxmantown Green; would suffer no man to rule here for the king, but himself?'

When Kildare died in 1513 he was still the virtual ruler of Ireland. His son succeeded him in office and the supremacy of the house of Kildare was maintained. But he was not the man his father had been, either in personality or military and diplomatic ability. The old Butler enmity was to be revived, new men in England were to resent the arrogance of the Kildare monopoly in Ireland, and the fatal involvement of other Geraldines, notably Desmond, with the enemies of England abroad were to turn the king against Kildare and break the hold of his family upon the government of Ireland. The death of the Great Earl, then, marked the end of an era. The new Ireland, shaped by the new men who supplied great military, administrative and diplomatic skills to the second Tudor king, could have no place for men like him. If in some ways he was a product of the renaissance, looking forward to a new age, in essence he was still typical of the lords of medieval Ireland. When he and his house passed from the political scene, the middle ages in Ireland had come to an end.

Glossary

assignment: the anticipation of revenue by means of a *tally* (q.v.) issued in advance of payment by some accountant at the exchequer.

barony: a local administrative division in the county. In the later middle ages tenure of a barony carried the right to be summoned to parliament.

betagh: the typical unfree tenant of the Irish manor, usually of Gaelic origin.

black rent: an illegal subsidy paid by many Anglo-Irish communities to a Gaelic lord in return for immunity from attack.

chancellor: the keeper of the Irish great seal, second in rank only to the chief governor and normally itinerating with him.

coyne and livery: the illegal exactions, in kind or money, to support troops quartered on the countryside, and the requisitioning of supplies.

crannock: a common Irish dry measure, usually equivalent to eight bushels, though like most medieval measures there was much variety according to local custom.

crossland: church lands within *liberties* (q.v.) which were reserved to the Crown and were outside the jurisdiction of the liberty.

fief (fee): usually land, granted to a tenant as an hereditary tenement in return for certain services, most commonly military.

great council: a parliamentary assembly, without the full dignity of a parliament.

indenture: a form of contract between two parties.

hobelar: a mounted archer, lightly armoured and riding a fast pony (a 'hobby').

land of peace: the area in which the king's law was maintained. Outside lay the *land of war*.

liberty: a fief which, with certain exceptions, lay outside the royal administration and jurisdiction.

march: the border lands which lay between the *land of war* and the *land of peace* (q.v.).

murage: a toll levied on certain goods entering towns for sale, to pay the cost of building or maintaining town walls.

ploughland: traditionally the area of land which could be ploughed in one day by a team of eight oxen. Normally 120 acres, it was also the area used for assessing parliamentary subsidies in the later middle ages.

purveyance: the king's right, delegated to the chief governor in Ireland, to preempt food and procure transportation for his household.

royal service: the Irish equivalent of English scutage, being the payment of money (fixed at the rate of 40s. for one knight) instead of performing military service in person.

sheriff: the royal official in charge of the shire (or county), which was the most important administrative division in local government.

tally: a small wooden stick, issued at the exchequer as a receipt for money paid in, with the amount shown by notches cut along the side.

writ: a written formal order from the king or his officials.

Bibliography

Abbreviations
IHS: *Irish Historical Studies*·
PRIA: *Proceedings of the Royal Irish Academy*
JRSAI: *Journal of the Royal Society of Antiquaries of Ireland.*

This is a highly selective list of works which is intended to provide a guide to anyone stimulated to further reading. Many of the works listed contain bibliographical sections or references which will lead the student on. Apart from the general section, I have arranged the bibliography to follow as closely as possible the different sections of each chapter. It will be immediately obvious that there are many areas of Irish history in the later middle ages which have been very badly served by historians. For an illumination of this see J. Otway-Ruthven, 'Medieval Ireland, 1169–1485', *IHS.*, xv (1967), 359–65. There is now available a very good critical bibliography of secondary works: P. W. Asplin, *Medieval Ireland, c. 1170–1495* (Dublin 1971). See also a much more selective bibliography in E. M. Johnston, *Irish History, a select bibliography* (revised edition London 1972).

General Works

The best general history of the period is still E. Curtis, *A history of medieval Ireland* (London 1938; reprinted 1968). The first edition (Dublin 1923) should also be consulted. Although failing to make best use of record sources and displaying sometimes an unfortunate ignorance of the medieval administration, Curtis had a natural sympathy with his subject and was also able to make use of a wide range of Gaelic sources. A. J. Otway-Ruthven, *A history of medieval Ireland* (London 1968) is now the best narrative and complements Curtis admirably. She is outstanding on government and institutions. G. H. Orpen, 'Ireland, 1315– c. 1485', *The Cambridge medieval history* (Cambridge 1936), 450–65, is a useful, short narrative. J. F. Lydon, *The Lordship of Ireland in the middle ages* (Dublin 1972) is a readable, thematic treatment and is a good introduction to the period. H. G. Richardson and G. O. Sayles, *The Irish parliament in the middle ages* (2nd. edn, Philadelphia 1964) covers a much wider field than the title suggests. It is a mine of information on political as well as financial and constitutional history, and is particularly valuable for the wide range of manuscript sources used. Some of the older histories contain sections which are still worth reading. J. T. Gilbert, *A history of the viceroys of Ireland* (Dublin 1865) is especially useful since it quotes from original sources, many of which have since been destroyed. A. G. Richey, *A short history of the Irish people* (edited by R. R. Kane, Dublin 1887) is a sadly neglected historian who is full of insights. K. Nicholls, *Gaelic and Gaelicised Ireland in the middle ages* (Dublin 1972) marks a real advance and is particularly valuable for a study of the Gaelic lordships and the institutions of Gaelic Ireland. G. Mac Gearailt, *Celt and Normans* (Dublin 1969) is a school text-book which has many superb illustrations not easily accessible elsewhere. Lord Killanin and M. V. Duignan, *Shell guide to Ireland* (2nd. edn, London 1967), is a magnificent, illustrated guide to the antiquities of Ireland and is a mine of useful information. P. Harbison, *Guide to the national monuments in the Republic of Ireland* (Dublin 1970) is lively and useful. The coins of medieval Ireland have recently been authoritatively and refreshingly treated by M. Dolley, *Medieval Anglo-Irish coins* (London 1972). In ecclesiastical architecture A. C. Champneys, *Irish ecclesiastical architecture* (Dublin 1910; reprinted Shannon 1970) is still the best. Volumes ii and iii of H. G. Leask, *Irish churches and monastic buildings* (Dundalk 1960) are more technical, with good plans and details illustrated. The most modern survey and by far the most stimulating, is R. A. Stalley, *Architecture and Sculpture in Ireland, 1150–1350* (Dublin 1971). H. G. Leask, *Irish Castles* (Dundalk 1951) is a good introduction to a neglected subject. For the Church see J. Watt, *The Church in medieval Ireland* (Dublin 1973) and the references cited there. A small but useful collection of sources is E. Curtis and R. B. MacDowell (eds.), *Irish Historical Documents, 1172–1922* (London 1943).

Chapter One

For the geography of Ireland, as depicted in maps, see T. J. Westropp, 'Early maps of Ireland', *PRIA.*, 30.C.No. 16 (1913), 361–428 (which is also very good on trade, shipping and the Irish ports). Medieval Ireland still awaits her economic historian, though a number of good papers will be found scattered in the journals. The second chapter of L. M. Cullen, *Life in Ireland* (London 1968) is by far the best introduction. The medieval section by D. A. Chart, *An economic history of Ireland* (Dublin 1920) is also good. For a typical Irish manor see J. O. Loan, 'The manor of Cloncurry, county Kildare,' *Department of Agriculture Journal*, lviii (1961), 14–36. There is also a good description in E. St John Brooks, 'Fourteenth century monastic estates in Meath: the Llanthony cells of Duleek and Colp', *JRSAI* lxxxiii (1953), 140–9; and E. Curtis, 'Rental of the manor of Lisronagh, 1333', *PRIA* 43C. No. 3 (1936) 41–76. The best account of agriculture is A. J. Otway-Ruthven, 'The organisation of Anglo-Irish agriculture in the middle ages', *JRSAI* lxxxi (1951), 1–13. Still of value is J. Mills, 'Tenants and agriculture near Dublin in the fourteenth century', *JRSAI* xxi (1890–91), 54–63 and 'Accounts of the earl of Norfolk's estates in Ireland, 1279–1294', *JRSAI* xxii

(1892), 50–62. Many of the accounts used by Mills may be read in translation in H. F. Hore, *Old and New Ross* (London 1900). This may be supplemented by J. Mills, *Account roll of the priory of the Holy Trinity, Dublin, 1337–1346* (Dublin 1891). Both of these make fascinating reading. On the general pattern of settlement the classic statement is A. J. Otway-Ruthven, 'The character of Norman settlement in Ireland' in J. L. McCracken (ed.), *Historical Studies V* (London 1965), 75–84. Two papers which inaugurate a whole new approach are by R. E. Glasscock, 'Ireland', in M. W. Beresford and J. G. Hurst (eds), *Deserted medieval villages* (London 1971), 279–301; and 'Moated sites, and deserted boroughs and villages' in N. Stephens and R. E. Glasscock (eds), *Irish geographical studies in honour of E. Estyn Evans* (Belfast 1970), 162–77. The second volume of G. Mac Niocaill, *Na Búirgéisí* (Dublin 1964) deals comprehensively with the medieval Irish towns. J. J. Webb, *Municipal government in Ireland* (Dublin 1918) is a good introduction. The same author's *The guilds of Dublin* (Dublin 1929) is the standard work. For a taste of the sources see J. T. Gilbert, *Calendar of the ancient records of Dublin* vol. i (Dublin 1890) and A. J. Otway-Ruthven's translation of the *Liber Primus Kilkenniensis* (Kilkenny 1961). E. M. Carus-Wilson, *Medieval merchant venturers* (London 1954) has a very good section on trade, as has the relevant chapters of W. O'Sullivan, *The economic history of Cork city* (London 1937). A. S. Green, *The making of Ireland and its undoing, 1200–1600* (London 1908) is still worth reading. For plays and pageants see A. Gwynn, 'The origins of the Anglo-Irish theatre', *Studies*, xxviii (1939), 260–74.

Chapter Two

The best general account is chapter V ('The government of the Norman-Irish state') of Otway-Ruthven's *History*. Essential as a work of reference is H. G. Richardson and G. O. Sayles, *The Administration of Ireland, 1172–1377*

(Dublin 1963) and, for a briefer account, their pamphlet *Parliament in Medieval Ireland* (Dundalk 1964). The same authors' book on parliament, listed earlier, is the standard account and is unlikely to be superseded. On taxation, in addition to the work of Richardson and Sayles, consult J. Lydon's papers 'The Irish church and taxation in the fourteenth century', *Irish Ecclesiastical Record*, 5th series, ciii (1965), 158–65; and 'William of Windsor and the Irish parliament', in *English Historical Review*, lxxx (1965), 252–67. H. G. Richardson and G. O. Sayles, 'Irish revenue 1278–1384', *PRIA* 62 C. No. 4 (1962), 87–100 is an important survey. Local government is a much neglected subject. A. J. Otway-Ruthven, 'Anglo-Irish shire government in the thirteenth century', *IHS* V (1946–7) is a good introduction. For a later period see D. B. Quinn, 'Anglo-Irish local government, 1485–1534', *IHS* i (1938–9), 354–81. The best introduction to the common law in Ireland is G. J. Hand, 'English law in Ireland, 1172–1351', *Northern Ireland Legal Quarterly*, 23 (1972), 393–422. The same journal (16–23) contains a fascinating, if brief, examination of the impact of one law on the other, by G. Mac Niocaill, 'The contact of Irish and common law'. A paper of great significance is B. Murphy, 'The status of the native Irish after 1331', *Irish Jurist*, new series, ii (1967), 116–38.

Chapter Three

Part IV of A. Gwynn and D. F. Gleeson, *A history of the diocese of Killaloe* is useful on the progress of the Gaelic revival in one part of Ireland, though it must be used with caution. E. Curtis, 'The clan system among English settlers in Ireland', *English Historical Review*, XXV (1910), 116–20 is a good introduction to the problem of hibernicisation. See also J. Lydon, 'The problem of the frontier in medieval Ireland', *Topic: a journal of the liberal arts*, 13 (1967), 5–22, for a broad discussion of the contact between two cultures. G. O. Sayles, 'The rebellious first earl of Desmond', in

J. Watt, J. B. Morrall and F. X. Martin (eds), *Medieval Studies presented to Aubrey Gwynn, S.J.* (Dublin 1961), 203–29, is a marvellously stimulating account of early fourteenth-century politics. R. G. Nicholson, 'An Irish expedition to Scotland in 1335', *IHS* xiii (1962–3), 197–211, is an outstanding account of the significance of the last major expedition to Scotland. On the Black Death A. Gwynn, 'The Black Death in Ireland', *Studies*, xxiv (1935), 25–42, is readable and informative. A. J. Otway-Ruthven, 'Ireland in the 1350s: Sir Thomas de Rokeby and his successors', *JRSAI* xcvii (1967), 47–59, is a detailed narrative of events during the years preceding the Clarence expedition.

Chapter Four

There is no satisfactory account, despite the super-abundance of sources, of the Clarence expedition. E. Curtis, 'The viceroyalty of Lionel, duke of Clarence, in Ireland 1361–1367', *JRSAI* xlvii (1917), 165–81, and xlviii (1918), 65–73, is too general to be of much use. There is a very good discussion on the statutes of Kilkenny, mainly from a technical viewpoint, by G. J. Hand, 'The forgotten statutes of Kilkenny', *Irish Jurist*, new series, i (1966), 299–312. The old edition of J. Hardiman, in *Tracts relating to Ireland printed for the Irish Archaeological Society*, ii (Dublin 1843), is still wonderfully useful for the riches of its notes. On William of Windsor the best account is still that of M. V. Clarke, 'William of Windsor in Ireland, 1369–1376', *PRIA* 41. C. No. 2 (1932), 55–130, reprinted in her *Fourteenth century studies* (London 1937). A most valuable contribution to the history of Anglo-Irish relations in the late fourteenth century is A. Tuck, 'Anglo-Irish relations, 1382–1393', *PRIA.*, 69 C. No. 2 (1970), 15–31. E. Curtis, *Richard II in Ireland* (Oxford 1927) prints, with translations, the texts of the submissions to the king and it also has a long historical introduction. His paper, 'Unpublished letters from Richard II in Ireland, 1394–5', *PRIA* 37. C. No. 14 (1927), also has a good general account and useful maps. J. Lydon, 'Richard II's expeditions to Ireland', *JRSAI* xciii (1963), 135–49, is the most modern account.

Chapter Five

The history of Ireland in the fifteenth century has been almost completely neglected. There are very good sections in J. H. Wylie, *History of England under Henry IV*, 4 vols (Oxford 1884–98), and J. H. Wylie and W. T. Waugh, *The reign of Henry V*, 3 vols (Oxford 1914–29). M. Griffith, 'The Talbot-Ormond struggle for control of the Anglo-Irish government, 1414–47', *IHS* ii (1940–41), 376–97, is a detailed account, with useful sources. J. H. Bernard, 'Richard Talbot, archbishop and chancellor, 1418–1449', *PRIA* 35 C. No. 5 (1919), 218–29, is a useful biography. H. G. Richardson, 'The Preston exemplification of the Modus tenendi parliamentum', *IHS* iii (1942–3), 187–92, is an important paper on a controversial subject. E. Curtis, 'Richard, duke of York, as viceroy of Ireland', *JRSAI* lxii (1932), 158–86, is a useful summary of the main facts, but is more important for the original documents it contains.

Chapter Six

The standard work on the Kildares is D. Bryan, *Gerald FitzGerald, the Great Earl of Kildare, 1456–1513*, (Dublin 1933), which is fairly reliable as a biography and contains much useful unpublished material. But as an interpretation it needs to be used with care. Richardson and Sayles provide a useful corrective in their book on parliament. A. Conway, *Henry VII's relations with Scotland and Ireland, 1485–1498* (Cambridge 1932) prints a mass of important administrative records and analyses in particular the mission of Poynings. It also contains a separate examination by E. Curtis of the legislation of Poynings' parliament. G. O. Sayles, 'The vindication of the earl of Kildare from treason, 1496', *IHS* vii (1950), 39–47, contains the best account of the relations between Poynings and Kildare. James Gairdner, *History of the life and reign of Richard III* (revised edition, Cambridge 1898) contains an excellent account of the Perkin Warbeck episode. Mary Hayden, 'Lambert Simnel in Ireland', *Studies*, iv (1915), 622–38, is a good short account. On Poynings' law see D. B. Quinn, 'The early interpretation of Poynings' law, 1494–1586', *IHS* ii (1940–1), 241–54; and R. D. Edwards and T. W. Moody, 'The history of Poynings' law. Part i. 1494–1615', *IHS* ii (1940–41), 415–24. The early pages of P. Wilson. *The beginnings of modern Ireland* (Dublin 1912) are still useful, as is the first part of R. Bagwell, *Ireland under the Tudors*, vol. i (London 1885).

Index

Abbeyknockmoy (co. Galway) 22
Ardfert (co. Kerry) 67
Armagh, archbishops of 139, 142, 161, 168
  council of 21, 33
Ashton, Robert 100, 104

Baltinglass (co. Wicklow) 33, 35
Barrow river 10, 92
Bristol 13, 14, 47, 108
Bruce, Edward and Robert, xi, xii, xiii, 40, 49–50, 61, 64, 73

Carlingford (co. Down) 63
Carlow 7, 42, 105, 175
  under Clarence 92–3, 96
  under earl of Kildare 154–5
  under Richard II 116–17, 121, 133
Cashel (co. Tipperary) 33
Castledermot (co. Kildare) 32
Chester 1, 89, 93
Clarence, Lionel duke of 52, 60, 65, 83, 84, 85, 87, 88–97, 105
Cloncurry (co. Kildare) 5, 7, 9
Clyn, Friar John 74, 77, 78, 79
Connacht 2, 42, 48, 55, 58, 62, 63, 99, 101, 165, 175
Connell (co. Kildare) 33, 35, 160
Cork xi, 42, 53, 65, 93, 105, 140
Courtenay, Sir Philip 105, 107
Coventry 47

Dalkey (co. Dublin) 4, 77
Darcy, John 44, 72
Dartmouth 46
de Barry, Gerald (Giraldus Cambrensis) 2, 21, 57
de Clare, Richard 62
de Courcy, John 28
de Geneville, Geoffrey 1
de Vere, Robert 86, 106, 107
Desmond, 1st earl of 54, 55–58, 73, 76, 82
  3rd earl of 107
  7th earl of 148, 149, 150

8th earl of 165
9th earl of 169, 170, 172, 173, 175, 179
Dingle (co. Kerry) 12
Drogheda (co. Louth) 9, 24, 63, 140, 178
  Black Death in 77
  council at 99
  parliament at 150, 161, 162, 177
Dublin xi, 33, 42, 92, 133
  Black Death in 77–8
  councils at 22, 23, 43–4, 70, 99
  exchequer 12, 37–8, 62–3, 93, 105
  government 27, 72, 74, 75, 83, 86, 126, 135, 138, 140, 143, 150, 157, 160–1, 172, 175
  Richard II in 116, 122–3
  sanitation 16–17
  Windsor in 97, 100, 103
Duleek (co. Meath) 8
Dundalk (co. Louth) xi, 136
Dysert O Dea (Clare) 61

Edgecombe, Sir Richard 167, 168
Edward I 1, 45, 49, 63
Edward II 49, 63, 178
Edward III 38, 49, 64, 83, 85–89, 96, 104
Edward IV 148–53, 159, 161, 162
Estrete, John 164

fitz Eustace, Sir Roland 150, 155, 160, 162, 172
fitz Ralph, Archbishop Richard 18, 79

Galway 2, 13, 15
Garth, Thomas 170, 172–3
Geraldines 54, 70, 135, 147, 148, 151, 152, 170, 172, 180
Gloucester, Thomas duke of 117, 123
  appointment to lordship 65, 108
  expeditions 70, 109
  revenue 86–7, 105
Grangegorman (co. Meath) 6
Grey, Henry Lord 30, 160–1